Helping Your Child to Learn
MATH

Helping Your Child to Learn MATH

by Gordon W. Green, Jr., Ph.D.

A Citadel Press Book
Published by Carol Publishing Group

For all students of mathematics who have
struggled and suffered because no one taught
them the fundamentals of the subject.

A Citadel Press Book
Published by Carol Publishing Group
Citadel Press is a registered trademark of Carol Communications, Inc.
Editorial Offices: 600 Madison Avenue, New York, N.Y. 10022
Sales and Distribution Offices: 120 Enterprise Avenue, Secaucus, N.J. 07094
In Canada: Canadian Manda Group, P.O. Box 920, One Atlantic Avenue,
    Suite 105, Toronto, Ontario M6K 3E7
Queries regarding rights and permissions should be addressed to Carol
    Publishing Group, 600 Madison Avenue, New York, N.Y. 10022

Carol Publishing Group books are available at special discounts for bulk
purchases, sales promotion, fund raising, or educational purposes.
Special editions can be created to specifications. For details, contact:
Special Sales Department, Carol Publishing Group, 120 Enterprise Avenue,
Secaucus, N.J. 07094

Manufactured in the United States of America
10 9 8 7 6 5 4 3 2 1

Library of Congress Cataloging-in-Publication Data

Green, Gordon W.
    Helping your child to learn math / by Gordon W. Green, Jr.
        p.   cm.
    A "Citadel Press book."
    ISBN 0-8065-1613-5 (pbk.)
    1. Mathematics—Study and teaching.   I. Title.
QA11.G776   1995
649'.68—dc20   94-43392
                                                            CIP

Contents

Preface

A Special Message for Parents (and Students)

When my daughter, Heidi, was taking her first semester of calculus in college, she was perplexed by a particular problem. I took a look at it and the examples in her textbook and said, "The explanation is right there in the textbook; did you read it?" She gave me a puzzled look and said, "Yes, I read it—several times in fact!—but it just doesn't make any sense to me." I looked at the problem again, and then realized that it would be very hard to understand for someone looking at it for the first time. The explanation was not all that clear, and seemed to be more complex than was necessary. To solve the problem was easy for me because I already knew how to do it.

"All right," I said. "Let's start over again. Forget about the book and just listen to me." I then proceeded to describe the problem in my own way, using words she was familiar with rather than the complex symbols normally associated with mathematical presentations. After explaining the concept, I then showed her what the mathematical symbols stood for and how to manipulate them properly. "Why, that's so simple!" she exclaimed. "Why didn't they just say so in the first place?" This is the same reaction I have heard from other students, including many in the earlier grades. They think that authors of mathematics books and teachers of the subject are making things unnecessarily difficult for them.

In the process of helping my daughter, I realized that many students have difficulty in understanding mathematical concepts because they do not understand the fundamentals, and the language of mathematics seems foreign to them. It is not, as is often assumed, that they do not have an aptitude for mathematics or that they are stupid. They may have failed to understand some crucial concept early in their study of mathematics and, consequently, much of the subsequent material is unnecessarily difficult for them. This is because mathematics is a very logical discipline in which just about everything builds on what was supposed to have been learned earlier. A good analogy is climbing a flight of stairs. If you go up the stairs one step at a time, you usually do not have any trouble. The problem often comes when you try to go up the stairs taking two or three steps at a time. You may stumble or fall. People encounter the same problem when they try to learn the more difficult concepts in mathematics after skipping over—or not fully understanding—the easier ones.

At one time or another, all parents have been approached by their children with requests for assistance on mathematics homework. All parents want to help, but many are rusty from not having taken the subject in many years. Moreover, the methods and notations used in today's textbooks may look different from the ones used when we took the subject a generation ago. In view of these considerations, I have set out to write a mathematics book that parents can use to explain basic concepts to their children in elementary and junior high school. Using this book from an early age will give youngsters a head start on the subject and make it easier for them to understand the concepts when they encounter them in the classroom. It also provides a very structured way for parents to explain concepts to their children in words that are easy to understand. The net result will be children who enjoy the subject because they already know a lot about it, and parents who are not frustrated or stressed out by frequent pleas for assistance from their children.

In this volume, I plan to cover many of the major topics in mathematics that students normally encounter at the elementary and junior high school levels. I am also writing a companion volume to this one, for high school and college students. That volume will cover a variety of topics suitable to students at those levels, including more advanced algebra, analytic geometry, functions, exponents and logarithms, trigonometry, and calculus.

It should be obvious to all that I cannot give an in-depth review in one volume of all of the topics in mathematics that students encounter in elementary and junior high school. I do not have the space to cover each of these areas exhaustively, or to provide a complete set of examples and problems that explore the various ramifications of each concept. But that is not my objective here. Readers can find an abundance of other books on mathematics that explore each field in depth. My objective is to teach the essence of each area of mathematics so the student will have a good foundation for understanding the subject when taking formal courses later on. Thus, this book should be viewed as a primer and supplement to other books on mathematics rather than as a replacement for them.

Why is a book like this needed? First of all, it should be clear to everyone that an understanding of mathematics is absolutely essential in today's world. Students are required to take courses in mathematics throughout their entire educational careers, and an in-depth understanding of the subject is needed to do well in college, especially in technical fields such as engineering, physics, computer science, economics, statistics, and so on. People trained in these fields will have access to the better jobs, in terms of both duties and pay, in our rapidly advancing technological world. Many students shy away from these fields because they are frightened to death by the mathematics required for them. An understanding of the fundamentals of mathematics makes these fields more accessible, improves academic performance, and makes the whole learning experience more enjoyable. If you think that a lot of mathematics is needed to function in our society today, then you should realize that even more will be required in the future.

Although I have directed this book to the parents, I have written it in a manner that I believe is also understandable to children. After receiving some help from their parents, children themselves should be able to pick up the book and understand the basic ideas of the various fields of mathematics, even though they may not encounter them until much later in their studies. Teachers may also find it useful as a supplement to their textbooks, particularly for students who are having difficulty understanding the basic ideas. As I noted earlier, mathematics builds on concepts learned earlier, so all readers will benefit by reading through the book from beginning to end rather than skipping around. If this book makes the subject of mathematics more understandable and enjoyable to parents and children alike, then I will have accomplished my objective.

Acknowledgments

My first debt of gratitude goes to Harold Roth, my literary agent, who has been trying for years to get me to write a book on mathematics. After I finally agreed to write the book, Harold was instrumental in convincing others that it was a worthwhile project. Without his patience and persistence, the book would still be a figment of my imagination. I am also indebted to all of the teachers of mathematics I have had during my entire educational career. The ones who had difficulty communicating their knowledge taught me how painful the subject can be for the student, and the ones who made everything crystal clear showed me that mathematics can be more enjoyable and enlightening than any subject in the curriculum. Through my experiences with them, I have learned a lot about the subject and have also gained an appreciation of the best way to teach it. Last, but not least, I wish to thank my dear wife, Maureen, who not only grants me the time to write books during my spare hours but also plays an active role in making sure that these projects are completed on time.

A mathematician, like a painter or a poet, is a maker of patterns. If his patterns are more permanent than theirs, it is because they are made with ideas.

—GODFREY HAROLD HARDY

A Mathematician's Apology

Helping Your Child to Learn
MATH

1

Introduction

Have you ever heard the phrase "math anxiety"? Well, everyone knows what math is, and anxiety means that you are scared, nervous, or tense. So math anxiety means that people are afraid of even the *thought* of having to do mathematics because they think they will fail. Their fear gets worse with each experience until they become scared about even coming into contact with the subject.

The first thing that parents need to do is explain to their children that "math anxiety" is something that most people experience at one time or another. The challenge is to confront our fears at an early stage and overcome them, so we can feel at ease with mathematics and clear the way to make progress in the subject. It might interest your child to know that even I, the author of a book on mathematics, was once a victim of "math anxiety." Here is a brief summary of my experiences, which you can relate to your youngster for encouragement.

I was afraid of math even in elementary and junior high school, but the feeling got worse in high school. Although it has been many years since then, I can remember walking into my high-school trigonometry class on the day of a big test. I had that uneasy feeling in my stomach, my knees were limp, and my heart was beating so rapidly in my throat that I could hardly breathe. Sound familiar? I hadn't really understood any of the material covered in the book or presented in class by the teacher. When I opened the exam it looked like Greek—in fact, many of the letters were in Greek!

I suffered through that hour with a stream of sweat running down my forehead, guessing wildly in the hope that I might get lucky. When the marked test was returned, it confirmed what I already knew: I got an F. And when my report card came at the end of the grading period, I was not surprised to discover that I had flunked the entire course. I hated mathematics more than anything in the world.

My dislike of mathematics followed me into college. When looking at the courses offered, I can remember shaking when I read that people studying economics had to take a certain number of math credits in order to graduate. I was not alone in my fear and anxiety. I can remember talking to some other students who were scared to death at the thought of having to take mathematics. "Don't worry," some students majoring in math told us. "With the easy courses you're taking, it will be a piece of cake." Well, it wasn't. Torture would be a more accurate description. The mathematical symbols became harder to understand, and the problems did not even seem to make sense. I was more confused than ever. But I knew that I had to get through or else. At the time "or else" meant telling my family I had failed and trying to get a good job after getting out of school. I worked as hard as I could. At night I dreamed about mathematical symbols and equations rather than the kinds of things college students usually dream about. With all of my effort, I managed to get a D. I was able to get through two more mathematics courses and graduate. "Thank God," I thought. "Free at last!"

Not quite. After getting out of college with a degree in economics, I went out to look for a job. One of the offers I got was to work for the federal government, in the U.S. Census Bureau. "What do you do here?" I asked my future boss during the job interview. "Well, we do a lot of things," he said, "but mostly we do statistics." I felt a sharp pain shoot through my spine. "Statistics—a close relative of mathematics," was the thought that ran through my brain. I guess he sensed from the worried look on my face that something wasn't quite right, because he asked, "Is something wrong?"

Thinking about my empty wallet and swallowing hard, I replied, "No, sir, not at all. I am fascinated by statistics." He looked at me with a smile on his face and said, "That's good, because you're going to see more numbers than there are stars in the sky."

He was right. I never saw so many numbers in my whole life! The U.S. Census Bureau is where most of the nation's statistics are produced—by the warehouseful. There are statistics on population, government, business, industry, and just about everything else you can think of. You name it and the Census Bureau has it. At first I felt like I was living in the cave of a monster, because of my fear of numbers. "My nightmare come true," I thought, "and all for a few lousy bucks!" But, miraculously, after a while I began to enjoy my work. Statistics about different subjects gave me a better understanding of what was going on in the world. I even started to take mathematics and statistics books home at night so I could discuss the concepts the next day with other people at the Census Bureau.

A few years later I made a courageous decision. I went back to college, at night, while working during the day, to take mathematics courses with students majoring in math. This time I was prepared for the challenge. I had learned some theory, had a lot of good practical experience, and was willing to work very hard. I was still scared, but I developed a system of study that worked like a charm. I took all of the difficult mathematics courses—differential calculus, integral calculus, linear algebra, calculus of several variables, and so on—and then went on to take courses in mathematical statistics. Afterwards I received a Ph.D. in economics, taking difficult quantitative courses like mathematical economics, econometrics, and operations research. During my "second" college career, I got A's not only in every course I took but also on every test I took. And to my surprise, getting A's in mathematics was easier than I had thought. I went on to write a book about my experiences, titled *Getting Straight A's*, which sold hundreds of thousands of copies, went into a new edition, was translated into Spanish, and now is in bookstores all around the world. Perhaps most amazing of all, I ended up spending my entire career as a professional statistician, even though I had hated and feared mathematics during my early years.

The situation I described earlier about "math anxiety" is not an unusual one. Most people are frightened of mathematics. Unfortunately, their stories usually do not have such a happy ending as does mine. They go through life without ever understanding the fundamentals of mathematics. Because of this, they might not get through college, might not get the job they want, and might not be able to train for another job if it requires mathematical knowledge. Many people fear that coworkers might learn about their ignorance of mathematics and worry that they might lose their job. In more serious cases there are people who do not know enough mathematics to accomplish daily activities, such as balancing their checkbooks or adding up their bills. The situation will only get worse, not better. People need to know more and more mathematics just to get by each day. When today's children grow up they will be required to know much more mathematics than did their parents. Why don't people who are ignorant of mathematics do something about it? The answer is very simple—they're frightened!

The best way to avoid the fear of mathematics is to learn it from a very early age. To show parents how to teach their youngsters mathematics, I have made this a very different kind of mathematics book. Instead of using a lot of complicated symbols, I have included plenty of plain English so you and they will know exactly what is going on. I have gone back to the fundamentals, so people with only a basic understanding of mathematics can start at the beginning and work their way through the entire book without difficulty. I do not cover every issue in each area of mathematics, only the basic ideas and some examples so you and your youngsters will have a good understanding of what each subject is about. There are no long exercises or difficult problems to solve. The examples I use illustrate the basic principles and show how they can be used to solve everyday problems. In summary, this is intended to be a short, practical book without any more complexity than is absolutely necessary. It should be a useful introduction to give children enough background to understand the basic ideas in different areas of mathematics. I am not trying to replace the textbooks. There are plenty of excellent mathematics textbooks already available. My goal is to supplement them.

The method that I plan to use in this book can be illustrated by the example of the first mathematics teacher I met when I returned to college for a "second" time. When teaching us calculus, he started at the beginning and said things that seemed very simple. What he said was so obvious that several of us in the class looked at each other and wondered why he would say something that was almost common sense. We continued to feel this way throughout the entire course since everything he said followed so clearly from what he had said before. By the end of the class we were amazed at how much we had learned when we looked back through our textbook. And it had all been so easy, even fun! This is the feeling that I hope you and your children will have when you finish reading this book.

In this book I plan to cover the following topics in mathematics: basic arithmetic, decimals, fractions, ratios, proportions, percents, weights and measures (including the metric system), geometry, algebra, and the graphing of equations. You are encouraged to read from the beginning, along with your children, so they will not miss anything needed later on. In this introduction, I will give a brief summary of the various topics that I will be covering in each of these areas of mathematics.

The starting point for understanding mathematics is to master basic arithmetic. Although your children may already be familiar with addition, subtraction, multiplication, and division, I review these subjects again to make sure that they know what they should know about these subjects. What many people fail to learn are the basic properties of arithmetic, such as the zero, identity, and commutative, associative, and distributive properties—and this is what gives them difficulty later on when they try to understand how these properties are used in algebraic expressions. I will review these basic properties and also discuss some problems that require the use of arithmetic.

Once your child understands how to perform basic arithmetic using whole numbers, the next task is to understand the concept of decimals. We use decimals to represent parts of numbers, so I show your youngster how to read different decimal positions such as tenths, hundredths, and thousandths. We then look at how to do basic arithmetic with decimals, such as adding, subtracting, multiplying, and dividing. All of the same rules of arithmetic apply. The only difference is knowing where to put the decimal point. I finish the chapter with a discussion of rounding and estimating, since these are things students often have to do when working with decimals.

Fractions are also used to show parts of numbers, and we represent them by a numerator divided by a denominator. I discuss some basic concepts, such as the least common multiple, the greatest common factor, and prime factorization. I then describe how to perform various operations on fractions, such as expressing them in their simplest form, converting between mixed numbers and ordinary fractions, and adding, subtracting, multiplying, and dividing fractions. These techniques are useful to children not only in working with fractions, but also for the later discussion on algebra.

I also discuss the related concepts of ratios, proportions, and percents. Here we will review the concept of an equation and show how to solve some very simple ones. I show that a ratio is just a way to compare two related numbers. Once your child knows what a ratio is, it should be easy for him or her to understand a proportion because it just says that two ratios are equal to each other. One of the most common measures we use every day is a percent, which is just a ratio that compares some number to a hundred. Children should be exposed to this concept very early.

Weights and measures are something that adults and children have to use just about every day of their lives. We all need to understand the concepts of time, temperature, length, weight, and volume. Although just about everyone knows these concepts almost as second nature, the difficulty often comes when they are asked to express them in metric units. It is important for all Americans to understand the metric scale, because it is the measure most often used in scientific work and in most of the rest of the world—and sooner or later, we will all have to know it anyhow! Parents often have difficulty teaching their children about this subject because they never studied it in school. I present a simple, easy-to-follow method to teach about the metric units of length (meter), capacity (liter), and mass (gram).

Geometry, which is derived from the ancient Greek word that means "to measure the earth," moves us from the world of numbers to physical representation. Many children like geometry because they can see physical representations of objects and ideas. I start off with basic concepts such as points, lines, rays, line segments, angles, and planes. These are the basic building blocks that are used to construct the geometrical figures that we usually associate with the word geometry—triangles, squares, rectangles, parallelograms, circles, and so forth. I also cover different relationships between geometrical figures, such as congruency, similarity, lines of symmetry, translation, rotation, and reflection. And, of course, I cover the concepts of perimeter and area for the basic geometric figures. I then discuss the Pythagorean theorem, named after the ancient Greek mathematician Pythagoras, which has a lot of practical applications. I conclude by discussing various three-dimensional (or solid) figures, such as cubes, prisms, pyramids, cones, cylinders, and spheres, and showing how to calculate the surface area and volume for these figures.

With algebra we are not only performing basic arithmetic

operations with numbers, but are also using letters to represent some of the numbers. Many children have difficulty with algebra because they were never taught the basics of the subject. I start with the basic idea of a number line, including positive and negative numbers, and then discuss various relationships such as less than, greater than, equal to, and the absolute value of a number. I then cover the various arithmetical properties of numbers—addition, subtraction, multiplication, and division—but now using algebraic expressions. I discuss powers and roots of numbers, and the proper order to follow when multiple operations are present in algebraic expressions. After this, I discuss operations involving polynomials, which are algebraic expressions having coefficients and variables raised to positive exponents. I also discuss solving equations with unknown values and inequalities, as well as what so many students fear—word problems. Factoring is a basic requirement for mastering algebra, so I cover it in detail and show some of its many applications, such as solving equations. I also review various operations involving algebraic fractions, since they occur quite frequently in higher mathematics, and seem to give children a lot of trouble. I close with a discussion of arithmetic operations involving square roots, and show how to solve quadratic equations.

Graphing is one of the most useful techniques in mathematics because it is used in many of its various fields. I start out with a description of the rectangular coordinate system, in which there is an x-axis and a y-axis in a plane, and show how to plot specific points in this plane. Then I show how to graph the equation of a straight line and explore the related concepts of intercepts and slope of the line. Using different forms of the equation for a straight line, I illustrate how to plot the graph when different sets of information are given. Finally, I conclude with a brief discussion of how to graph curved lines and inequalities.

*   *   *

I realize that many of the words and mathematical concepts that I have discussed in this introduction are probably unfamiliar to you and your children, and that is okay. I only mention them at this point because I want you both to know the direction we will be taking and all of the interesting things your children will know by the end of this book. I have tried to present everything so it follows very naturally in order. This means that you and your children should be able to pick up this book and read it straight through. If you skip around, your children will probably have more trouble because they might have missed what came before. Always instill in them that mathematics is one of the most interesting and enjoyable subjects they can study in school, and my deepest hope is that they will agree with you after you both have finished this book!

2

Basic Arithmetic

Basic arithmetic is not only something that we need in order to function every day in our society, it is the foundation for all other topics in mathematics. Our parents recognize the importance of basic arithmetic because they start us off with learning how to count on our fingers from the earliest age. At first we simply repeat the word associated with each number, and gradually we learn how to write the symbol that corresponds to each number. After we reach amounts that extend beyond our number of fingers (and possibly toes), we need another method for representing numbers. So we learn how to express larger numbers in groups of three, corresponding to ones, thousands, millions, billions, trillions, and so forth. For example, you can show your child how to express the number 300 billion, 410 million, 652 thousand, 934 as:

Billions			Millions			Thousands			Ones		
hundred billions	ten billions	billions	hundred millions	ten millions	millions	hundred thousands	ten thousands	thousands	hundreds	tens	ones
3	0	0,	4	1	0,	6	5	2,	9	3	4

After we learn how to count on our fingers, the next concept we are usually introduced to is addition. At first we learn how to combine numbers of fingers together to get a larger number, and then we learn basic facts such as that two fingers plus two fingers equals four fingers. Very quickly we encounter numbers larger than our total number of fingers, so we need another way to understand addition for larger numbers. Actually, we have implicitly introduced the concept of addition even when we express a number. For example, you can point out to your youngster that the number 652 thousand, 934 is merely the sum of the following numbers:

$$652,934 = 600,000 + 50,000 + 2,000 + 900 + 30 + 4$$

Comparing Numbers

The next thing we usually learn is how to compare two (or more) numbers to see if they are greater than (>), less than (<), or equal to (=) each other. This is performed by lining up the digits of the numbers and comparing them from left to right. The first place where they differ indicates the relative size of the numbers. For example, to show your child how to compare the following numbers,

652,934
651,876
98,999

stress that 652,934 is greater than 651,876 because the former has a larger digit (2) than the latter (1) in the first place they differ. The number 98,999 is the smallest because it has no hundred thousands. Thus, we can write the following relationships about these numbers:

652,934 > 651,876	or	651,876 < 652,934
652,934 > 98,999	or	98,999 < 652,934
651,876 > 98,999	or	98,999 < 651,876

Addition

In performing the operation of addition, it is very important for students to learn and remember some basic properties. Many people have difficulty later on in mathematics because they have failed to learn these properties. With addition, of course, we are just combining numbers together to arrive at a total amount. For example, if I have three of something and five of something, the total number I have is eight. In making calculations such as this it is important for children to know the following basic properties of addition:

Addition Properties

Identity Property
If zero is added to any number, $3 + 0 = 3$
the sum is equal to the number. $0 + 5 = 5$

Commutative Property
If the order of numbers added $3 + 5 = 5 + 3$
together is changed, the result $8 = 8$
(sum) stays the same.

Associative Property
If the grouping of numbers is $(2 + 1) + 5 = 2 + (1 + 5)$
changed, the sum remains the $\downarrow$ $\downarrow$
same. $3 \quad + 5 = 2 + \quad 6$
                                              $8 = 8$

When children are asked to add up a series of numbers, it is important for them to know how to line the numbers up in a column to perform the operation. For example, suppose I have 230 red marbles, 467 white marbles, and 763 blue marbles, and I want to know how many marbles I have altogether. I would add the numbers together by performing the following steps:

Add up the ones and regroup, if necessary.	Add up the tens and regroup, if necessary.	Add up the hundreds and regroup, if necessary.	Check the sum by adding up the numbers.
1	11	11	11 ↑
230	230	230	230
467	467	467	467
+ 763	+ 763	+ 763	+ 763
0	60	1460	1460

I have 1,460 marbles altogether.

Subtraction

With subtraction, emphasize to students that they are just comparing two numbers to see how many more are left or how many more are needed. A knowledge of addition helps in understanding subtraction. For example, if I want to know the result of five take away (minus) three, I only need to ask myself, "What number added to three equals five?" The result (or difference), of course, is just two. When performing the operation of subtraction, it is important to remember that:

Subtraction Properties

If zero is subtracted from any number, the result (difference) is just the number.	$3 - 0 = 3$ $5 - 0 = 5$
When any number is subtracted from itself, the difference is always zero.	$3 - 3 = 0$ $5 - 5 = 0$
Subtraction, unlike addition, is not commutative.	$5 - 3 = 2$ $3 - 5 \neq 2$

(where $\neq$ means not equal to)

When subtracting one number from another, tell children that the numbers must be lined up properly in a column and regrouped by borrowing from the next largest column, if necessary. For example, if I have 695 marbles and want to know how many I have left if I sell 478 of them, I would subtract 478 from 695 as follows:

Regroup the numbers and subtract the ones.	Subtract the tens.	Subtract the hundreds.	Check the result by adding.
8 15	8 15	8 15	1
69̸5̸	69̸5̸	69̸5̸	478
−478	−478	−478	+217
7	17	217	695

I would have 217 marbles left for myself.

It is important to show your youngster that some extra steps are required when subtracting numbers that have zeros in them. In this case, it may be necessary to regroup the numbers more than once before performing the subtraction. For example, suppose that I carry marbles in my store, and out of a shipment of 4,400 I sell 3,156. I can find out how many I have left by going through the following steps:

Regroup the hundreds.	Regroup the tens.	Perform the subtraction.	Check the result by adding.
	9	9	
3 10	3 10 10	3 10 10	
44̸0̸0̸	44̸0̸0̸	44̸0̸0̸	3156
−3156	−3156	−3156	+1244
		1244	4400

I have 1,244 marbles left from my shipment.

Multiplication

As children we are all taught certain multiplication facts, such as one times one equals one, two times two equals four, three times three equals nine, and so forth. Most people try to commit to memory all multiplications of numbers up to twelve. The result is called a "times table," which I have included in Appendix A just in case any readers have forgotten any of the multiplications. Actually, the operation of multiplication can best be explained to children as a simple extension of addition. For example, if I have four things in one group, four more things in another group, and still four more things in another group, I can find out how many things I have by adding up the four in each of the three groups. Or, of course, I could simply multiply the number in each group (four) by the number of groups (three). Each number to be multiplied is called a factor, and the result is called the product. Before demonstrating some simple operations involving multiplication, it will be useful to review some basic properties that make multiplication easier to perform. These will be helpful to children later on when we discuss algebra.

Multiplication Properties

Identity Property
If one of the factors is 1, the product equals the other factor. $3 \times 1 = 3$ $1 \times 5 = 5$

Zero Property
If one of the factors is 0, the product equals 0. $6 \times 0 = 0$ $0 \times 4 = 0$

Commutative Property
If factors are multiplied in a different order, the product is still the same. $9 \times 7 = 63$ $7 \times 9 = 63$

Associative Property

If the factors are grouped together differently, the product is still the same.

$$(3 \times 4) \times 5 = 3 \times (4 \times 5)$$
$$\downarrow \qquad\qquad\qquad \downarrow$$
$$12 \quad \times 5 = 3 \times \quad 20$$
$$60 = 60$$

Distributive Property

To multiply a factor by the sum of two numbers, multiply the factor by each number separately, and then add the two products.

$$5 \times (6 + 7) = (5 \times 6) + (5 \times 7)$$
$$\downarrow \qquad\qquad \downarrow \qquad\qquad \downarrow$$
$$5 \times \quad 13 \quad = \quad 30 \quad + \quad 35$$
$$65 \quad = \quad 65$$

With these basic properties in mind, students should find it easier to solve a variety of problems involving multiplication. To begin, you can show your child how to multiply a number by a one-digit factor. Suppose each day I plant 528 flowers in a row along a walkway. How many flowers will I have planted during a three-day period? To find the answer we should multiply 528 by 3:

Multiply the ones and regroup the 2 tens.	Multiply the tens and then add the 2 tens.	Multiply the hundreds.
2	2	2
528	528	528
$\times$ 3	$\times$ 3	$\times$ 3
4	84	1584

I have planted 1,584 flowers in all.

Once children know how to multiply by a 1-digit factor, it is a simple matter to extend the concept to multiply by a 2-digit factor. The only additional requirement is knowing how to stack the rows associated with each digit so they can add to get the overall total. Now suppose that I own a tree nursery, and I have 56 different groups of trees with 24 trees in each group. How many trees do I have altogether? Here we need to multiply 56 by 24:

Multiply by ones.	Multiply by tens.	Add the rows.
56	56	56
$\times 24$	$\times 24$	$\times 24$
224	224	224
	112	112
		1344

I have 1,344 trees in my nursery.

Multiplication by 3-digit factors is also a simple extension, because all your youngster needs to do is perform another multiplication for the hundreds, which results in another row to add. Suppose I buy my trees from a company that grows them on a large plot of land. If the company has 693 trees in a row by 497 rows deep, how many trees does it grow altogether? To find the answer I need to multiply 693 by 497:

Multiply by ones.	Multiply by tens.	Multiply by hundreds.	Add the rows.
693	693	693	693
$\times 497$	$\times 497$	$\times 497$	$\times 497$
4851	4851	4851	4851
	6237	6237	6237
		2772	2772
			344421

The company grows a total of 344,421 trees.

Children should know that a special case involving multiplication occurs when one of the factors has one or more zeros at the end of it. In this case the trailing zeros of the factor should be shifted to the right before performing the multiplication. To illustrate, suppose we want to multiply 375 by 10, 100, and 1,000. The multiplications would be performed as follows:

Multiplication by 10.	Multiplication by 100.	Multiplication by 1,000.

$$\begin{array}{r} 375 \\ \times\ \ 10 \\ \hline 3750 \end{array}$$ $$\begin{array}{r} 375 \\ \times\ \ 100 \\ \hline 37500 \end{array}$$ $$\begin{array}{r} 375 \\ \times\ \ 1000 \\ \hline 375000 \end{array}$$

Division

Explain to students that in a similar way that subtraction is the opposite of addition, division is the opposite of multiplication. Your youngster can see this from looking at the TIMES TABLE in Appendix A. Take any product in the table and divide it by one of the factors, and the result is the other factor. There are three basic ways to represent division. To illustrate them, suppose we want to divide 48 by 6. This can be represented by:

$$48 \div 6 = 8 \qquad 6\overline{)48}^{\,8} \qquad \frac{48}{6} = 8$$

In the above representations, 48 is referred to as the dividend, 6 is called the divisor, and 8 is known as the quotient.

There are several important rules for students to remember when carrying out division:

Division Properties

When any number is divided by 1, the result is equal to the number.	$5 \div 1 = 5$
When any number (except 0) is divided by itself, the result is equal to 1.	$3 \div 3 = 1$
Division of a number by 0 is not allowed. (If $7 \div 0 =$ some number n, then $n \times 0 \neq 7$; it doesn't make sense.)	$7 \div 0$ not defined

When 0 is divided by another number (except 0), the result is 0.

$$0 \div 4 = 0$$

Children need to recognize that not all divisions come out as neatly as the ones presented above. Very often the numbers do not go into each other exactly, and there are other numbers (remainders) left over. To illustrate, suppose I have 51 baseball cards and I want to organize them into groups of 6. How many groups will I have, and how many cards will be left over?

```
   8 R3
6)51        The largest number that 6 will go into 51 is 8.
  48        Multiply 8 times 6 to get 48.
   3        Subtract 48 from 51 to get 3.
            Since 3 < 6, the remainder (R) is 3.
```

I will have 8 groups of cards, with 6 cards to a group and 3 left over.

Point out to children that when a number can be divided exactly by another number without a remainder, it is said to be divisible by that number. The above example illustrates division by a 1-digit divisor.

Sometimes we encounter situations where we need to divide larger numbers by a 1-digit divisor. For example, suppose that a company produces 3,274 bars of candy and puts them in packages containing 8 bars to sell at Halloween. How many packages can the company make, and how many candy bars will be left over?

To solve this problem we need to divide 3,274 by 8:

Divide the hundreds first. Think about 32 ÷ 8. Multiply 4 × 8, then subtract and compare.	Next divide the tens. Bring down the 7. Since 8 will not go into 7, write 0 in the quotient, multiply, subtract, and compare.	Now divide the ones. Bring down the 4. Think about 74 ÷ 8. Write 9 in the quotient, multiply, subtract, and compare.

$$\begin{array}{r} 4 \\ \hline 8)\overline{3,274} \\ 3\,2 \end{array}$$

$$\begin{array}{r} 40 \\ \hline 8)\overline{3,274} \\ 3\,2 \downarrow \\ 7 \\ 0 \\ \hline 7 \end{array}$$

$$\begin{array}{r} 409 \text{ R } 2 \\ \hline 8)\overline{3,274} \\ 3\,2 \\ 7 \\ 0 \downarrow \\ 74 \\ 72 \\ \hline 2 \end{array}$$

The company can produce 409 packages of candy and will have 2 bars left over.

Emphasize to children that they can check the accuracy of the computation by multiplying the quotient times the divisor, plus any remainders. If the division is correct, the result will equal the dividend. To illustrate:

Check.	409	(quotient)
	× 8	(divisor)
	3,272	
	+ 2	(remainder)
	3,274	(dividend)

It is a simple matter for your youngster to extend this approach to division by a 2-digit divisor. Now suppose that the candy company produces 53,976 bars of candy and puts 96 bars (or 12 packages containing 8 bars each) in a box. How many boxes of candy can the company produce, and how many bars will be left over? Here we need to divide 53,976 by 96:

Divide the hundreds first, since 96 will not go into 53. To estimate 539 ÷ 96, think about 53 ÷ 9. Try 5, then multiply, subtract, and compare. Since 59 < 96, 5 is a good choice. 4 would have been too small and 6 too large.

Divide the tens next. Since 59 < 96, bring down the 7. To estimate 597 ÷ 96, first think about 59 ÷ 9. Try 6, then multiply, subtract, and compare. Since 21 < 96, 6 is a good choice.

Now divide the ones. Since 21 < 96, bring down the 6 to get 216. To estimate 216 ÷ 96, think about 21 ÷ 9. Try 2, then multiply, subtract, and compare. Since 24 < 96, 24 is the remainder.

$$
\begin{array}{r}
5 \\
96\overline{)53,976} \\
48\,0 \\
\hline
5\,9
\end{array}
\qquad
\begin{array}{r}
56 \\
96\overline{)53,976} \\
48\,0 \downarrow \\
\hline
5\,97 \\
5\,76 \\
\hline
21
\end{array}
\qquad
\begin{array}{r}
562 \text{ R } 24 \\
96\overline{)53,976} \\
48\,0 \\
\hline
5\,97 \\
5\,76 \downarrow \\
\hline
216 \\
192 \\
\hline
24
\end{array}
$$

The company can produce 562 boxes of candy, and will have 24 bars left over.

Emphasize to children that no matter how carefully they have performed their calculations, it is always a good idea to check their work to make sure that it is accurate.

$$
\begin{array}{rl}
\text{Check.} & \ \ 562 \quad \text{(quotient)} \\
& \times \ \ \ \ 96 \quad \text{(divisor)} \\
\hline
& \ 3372 \\
& 5058 \\
\hline
& 53952 \\
& + \ \ \ \ 24 \quad \text{(remainder)} \\
\hline
& 53976 \quad \text{(dividend)}
\end{array}
$$

Your child should now have the hang of division by "long hand." Just to make sure, I will illustrate a division using a 3-digit divisor. Rather than going through separate steps, I will show one combined calculation, with explanations. Suppose a resort town has 928,195 visitors during the year. On average, how many visitors visit the town each day? Since there are 365 days in a year, we need to divide 928,195 by 365:

$$
\begin{array}{r}
2\ 543 \\
365\overline{)928{,}195} \\
730 \\
\overline{198\ 1} \\
182\ 5 \\
\overline{15\ 69} \\
14\ 60 \\
\overline{1\ 095} \\
1\ 095 \\
\overline{0}
\end{array}
$$

Since 365 will go into 928, the first digit of the quotient (2) goes into the thousands place. From there, we multiply, subtract, and compare, as in previous examples, bringing down digits from the dividend, as necessary. Since there is no remainder in this problem, the dividend is divisible by the divisor.

Check.

$$
\begin{array}{r}
2543 \\
\times\ 365 \\
\hline
12715 \\
15258 \\
7629 \\
\hline
928195
\end{array}
$$

Thus, the town has an average of 2,543 visitors a day.

Sometimes children will encounter problems in which both the dividend and divisor are numbers that are multiples of 10. In such cases, your child should eliminate an equal number of zeros (as many as possible) from both the dividend and divisor before performing the division. To illustrate, suppose we want to divide 68,000 by 400. To do this, we should strike two zeros from both the dividend and divisor, and then proceed as before.

$$
\begin{array}{r}
17\ 0 \\
400\overline{)68{,}000} \\
4 \\
\overline{28} \\
28 \\
\overline{0}
\end{array}
$$

Check.

$$
\begin{array}{r}
170 \\
\times\ 400 \\
\hline
68000
\end{array}
$$

Rounding and Estimating

It is important to explain to students that rounding and estimating are useful techniques for several reasons. Sometimes we do not need a precise answer, and an estimate that we can calculate in our heads will do just fine. Even when we need a precise answer, it is useful to be able to do some mental arithmetic to get an idea of what our answer should look like. We can compare this estimate against the result of our more formal arithmetic to tell whether or not it is reasonable.

Here is a good way to explain rounding to children. To round a number to a given place, we merely look at the next smaller digit. If this digit is equal to 5 or more, we increase the number in the given place by 1. If the next smaller digit is less than 5, then we keep the number in the given place the same. All of the digits after the given place become 0, so we get a rounded number. To illustrate, suppose we want to round the number 28,734,306 to millions.

First find the millions place.	Next look at the digit in the hundred thousands place.	If the hundred thousands digit is 5 or more, round up; if it is less than 5, round down.
28,734,306 ↑	28,734,306 ↑	28,734,306 $\overbrace{}$ 7 > 5, round up

The number, rounded to millions, is 29,000,000. In a similar manner, if we rounded to thousands, the result would be 28,734,000, because the next smaller digit in the hundreds place (3) is less than 5.

To give youngsters a simple illustration of the value of rounding, if they were asked to divide 4,023 by 395, they could do some quick mental arithmetic to round 4,023 to 4,000 and 395 to 400. They could then easily see that the approximate answer is 10 (4,000 divided by 400). Even if they did the calculation using long-hand division, they would know beforehand that the answer should not be too different from 10.

Summary

I realize that, in today's world, most people rely on calculators and computers—not pencils!—to do their arithmetic. Nonetheless, it is still useful for everyone to have the knowledge and facility to do basic arithmetic. It forms the foundation for everything else that follows in mathematics. By doing basic arithmetic in their formative years, and later on in their everyday activities, children develop definite opinions concerning how they feel about mathematics. Learning to do basic mathematics well helps reinforce the positive feelings.

3

Decimals

So far we have discussed basic arithmetic involving whole numbers. Whole numbers are suitable for solving many problems, but children must realize that sometimes we need more precise estimates. This moves us into the world of decimals, where it is possible to talk about units much smaller than whole numbers. Just as we talk about ones, tens, hundreds, thousands, and so on with whole numbers, we talk about tenths, hundredths, thousandths, and so on with decimals. The only difference is that now we are placing a decimal point after the ones position, and we are talking about portions of whole numbers that lie to the right of this decimal point. To illustrate this concept, we will use the following chart to talk about the number 352.48075:

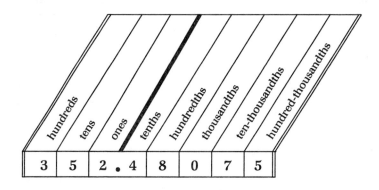

Point out to your child that the decimal point is between the ones and tenths position. The numbers to the left of the decimal point are whole numbers, and should be interpreted in the same way as numbers shown in the chart in the previous chapter. This tells us that there are 3 hundreds, 5 tens, and 2 ones, or 352. To the right of the decimal point there are 4 tenths, 8 hundredths, 0 thousandths, 7 ten-thousandths, and 5 hundred-thousandths. We say that this number is shown to 5 significant decimal places, because we show numbers to hundred-thousandths (count the number of places to the right of the decimal point). It would, of course, have been possible to show the number to more significant decimal places, such as millionths, ten-millionths, and so on, but we have not done so for the purposes of this illustration. Generally speaking, more significant places are needed when more precision is required.

It is important for students to understand that decimals are used to represent part of a whole. If we take a square representing one unit and divide it into ten equal parts, then each part is a tenth. In the number 352.48075 there are four tenths, so we could represent this by four shaded parts. If we take the square and divide it into one hundred equal parts, then each part is one hundredth of the whole. In the number 352.48075 there are forty-eight hundredths, so we could represent this by forty-eight shaded parts. By further dividing the square into additional equal parts, we could represent thousandths, ten-thousandths, and so on, but it gets difficult to represent graphically. In the number 352.48075 there are 352 whole units (or squares) and 48,075 hundred-thousandths of a unit (or square).

Square divided into tenths.

Square divided into hundredths.

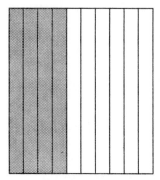

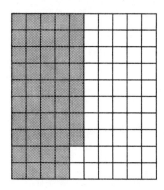

Four tenths shaded.

Forty-eight hundredths shaded.

Comparing Decimals

It is very important for children to be able to compare a set of numbers involving decimals and determine which numbers are larger or smaller than the others. As an example, suppose that three runners are trying out for the track team, and they have a race to see which one finishes first in running one lap around the track. The times of the three runners are: 58.76 seconds, 58.721 seconds, and 58.792 seconds. What is the fastest and slowest time of the runners? We can think about this problem by representing the numbers from lowest to highest on a number line:

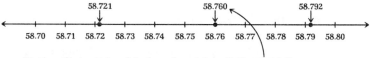

Notice that a 0 is added to the right of 58.76. Adding zeros after the right of the number does not change the value of the decimal.

Since 58.721 seconds is to the left of the other two numbers, it is the smallest number and hence the fastest time around the track. Also, 58.792 seconds is the largest number and hence the slowest time around the track. Using the symbols we learned earlier, we would say:

$$58.721 < 58.760 < 58.792$$

Emphasize to youngsters that they need a way to compare decimals that is more convenient than ordering them along a number line. The following approach shows them how to do this. Using the numbers from the example above:

First line the numbers up along the decimal point. Add zeros where necessary.	Next, comparing from the left, find the first place where the numbers differ.	Then continue to compare the numbers.

58.760	58.7**6**0 ⎫ This is the	Since 6 < 9
58.721	58.7**2**1 ← ⎬ smallest	58.760 < 58.792
58.792	58.7**9**2 ⎭ number.	

This approach gives the same result: $58.721 < 58.760 < 58.792$

Adding Decimals

You can continue with the same example to show your child how to add numbers with decimals.

The runner with the fastest time took 58.721 seconds to run one lap around the track. On three more laps, the same runner records times of 61.739 seconds, 64.94 seconds, and 68.073 seconds. How long did it take the runner to run all four laps around the track?

First line up the decimal points. Add zeros where appropriate.	Next add the decimals. Regroup where necessary.	Then add the whole numbers and write the decimal point.

		2 11	22 11
58.721		58.721	58.721
61.739	⎰ Add 0	61.739	61.739
64.940	⎱ after 4.	64.940	64.940
+ 68.073		+ 68.073	+ 68.073
		473	253.473

It took the runner 253.473 seconds to run all four laps.

Subtracting Decimals

Tell your child that we subtract numbers with decimals when we want to compare amounts or find out how much larger one number is than another. Continuing with the same example, we found that the first runner completed four laps in 253.473 seconds. If it took the second runner 264.49 seconds to run four laps, how much faster did the first run than the second? Here we need to subtract 253.473 from 264.49:

First line up the decimal points and add zeros where necessary.	Next regroup the numbers and subtract the decimals.	Then subtract the whole numbers and add the decimal.

		8 10	8 10
264.490	⎰ Add 0	264.490	264.490
− 253.473	⎱ after 9.	− 253.473	− 253.473
		017	11.017

This zero must be shown here.

The first runner ran the laps 11.017 seconds faster than the second runner.

One further illustration for students to understand subtracting numbers with decimals: If the third runner ran the four laps in 270 seconds flat, how much faster did the first run than the third? For this, we need to subtract the time of the first runner (253.473 seconds) from the time of the third runner (270 seconds). Everything should be set up as before, except now we need to add a decimal point and three zeros after the whole number 270:

First line up the decimal points and add zeros where necessary.	Next regroup the numbers and subtract the decimals.	Then subtract the whole numbers and add the decimal.
	9 9	9 9
	6 9 10 10 10	6 9 10 10 10
270.000	270.000	270.000
− 253.473	− 253.473	− 253.473
	527	16.527

The first runner ran the laps 16.527 seconds faster than the third runner.

Multiplying Decimals

Children should be aware that some problems require them to multiply numbers containing decimals. We will start off with an example that requires multiplication of a number containing a decimal by a whole number. Suppose that I am going on a camping trip with a group of friends, and my job is to figure out how much food will be needed on the trip. Rather than buy food in boxes I decide to buy in bulk to save space. I estimate that the group will need 3.75 pounds of cereal a day, for each of the 6 days of the trip. How much cereal should I purchase altogether? To solve this problem I need to multiply 3.75 by 6:

First multiply out all of the digits.	The product will have the same number of decimal places that appear in the two factors combined.

3.75	3.75 ←—— two decimal places
× 6	× 6 ←—— no decimal places
22 50	22.50 ←—— two decimal places

I will need 22.50 pounds of cereal altogether.

Sometimes it is necessary to add leading zeros to the product in order to put the decimal point in the correct place. This is often the case when at least one of the factors is a very small number. For example, suppose I want to multiply .0037 by 26. I would proceed as follows:

First multiply out all of the digits.	Make sure the product has the same number of decimal places as the factors. Add leading zeros.

.0037	.0037 ←—— four decimal places
× 26	× 26 ←—— no decimal places
222	222
74	74
962	.0962 ←—— four decimal places
	↑
	⎣—— one leading zero

Here is an example for your child to see what happens when both factors have decimal places. As noted, it is important that the product have the same number of decimal places as both factors. We will also introduce the concept of money, which is nothing more than a number containing decimals that go only to the level of hundredths (cents). Returning to our example of the camping trip, suppose the cereal costs $1.95 a pound. How much will my 22.50 pounds of cereal cost? Here I need to multiply 22.50 by $1.95. Since zeros to the right of a number do not change the value of a decimal, we can simply multiply 22.5 by $1.95:

First multiply out all of the digits.

Make sure that the product has the same number of decimal places as both factors combined.

$$\begin{array}{r} \$1.95 \\ \times\ \ 22.5 \\ \hline 975 \\ 390 \\ \underline{390} \\ 43875 \end{array}$$

$\$1.95$ ⟵── two decimal places
$\times\ \ 22.5$ ⟵── + one decimal place
975
390   equals
$\underline{390}$
$\$43.875$ ⟵── three decimal places

Since the problem involves money, I need to express the answer in dollars and cents. Thus, I need to round the answer up to $43.88. (I will say more on rounding and estimating with decimals at a later point.)

It is important for children to know that there are many occasions when they need to multiply numbers with decimals by a factor of 10, 100, or 1,000. In such cases, all they need to do is move the decimal point one place to the right for each zero in the factor they are multiplying by. To illustrate this concept, we will multiply 8.734 by 10, 100, and 1,000:

$8.734 \times 10 = 87.34$ ⟵── Move the decimal point one place to the right.

$8.734 \times 100 = 873.4$ ⟵── Move the decimal point two places to the right.

$8.734 \times 1000 = 8734.$ ⟵── Move the decimal point three places to the right.

The same approach applies to money. For example, to multiply $43.88 by 100:

$\$43.88 \times 100 = \$4388.$ ⟵── Move the decimal point two places to the right.

Dividing Decimals

Just as children need to perform division involving whole numbers, there are also many times when they need to do division with decimals. The principles of both are exactly the same. The only difference is that they need to know how to place the decimal point when working with numbers that have decimals.

You will start off with an example involving division of a decimal by a whole number. If it takes exactly 8 gallons of gas for me to drive my car to the beach, and the trip is 220.8 miles long, how many miles am I getting to the gallon? Here I need to divide 220.8 by 8:

First set up the problem and put the decimal point in the quotient.	Next divide the whole numbers—the tens and the ones.	Then divide the decimals—the tenths.

$$
\begin{array}{r} . \\ 8\overline{)220.8} \end{array}
\qquad
\begin{array}{r} 27. \\ 8\overline{)220.8} \\ \underline{16}\downarrow \\ 60 \\ \underline{56} \\ 4 \end{array}
\qquad
\begin{array}{r} 27.6 \\ 8\overline{)220.8} \\ \underline{16} \\ 60 \\ \underline{56}\downarrow \\ 4\,8 \\ \underline{4\,8} \\ 0 \end{array}
$$

I got 27.6 miles to the gallon on my trip to the beach.

Point out to students that sometimes they need to add zeros to the dividend in order to carry out the division. For example, I know that my truck does not get as good mileage as my car. If I drive my truck 98.1 miles to the mountains, and it takes 6 gallons of gas to get there, then how many miles to the gallon am I getting on my truck? Here I need to divide 98.1 by 6:

First put the decimal in the quotient and divide the whole numbers.

Next divide the tenths. Notice that there is a remainder.

Now add a zero to the dividend and divide the hundredths.

```
      16.                   16.3                  16.35
  6)98.1                6)98.1               6)98.10
    6                     6                    6
    38                    38                   38
    36                    36                   36
     2                     2 1                  2 1
                           1 8                  1 8
                             3                   30
                                                 30
                                                  0
```

I got 16.35 miles to the gallon driving my truck to the mountains.

When we divide a decimal by a decimal, we have to shift the decimal point to make the divisor a whole number. Suppose that a train only gets .84 miles to a gallon of diesel fuel, and I want to know how many gallons of fuel are required for a trip that is exactly 47.04 miles long. Divide 47.04 by .84

First shift the decimal point in the divisor and dividend two places to the right.

Next put the new decimal point in the quotient.

Then perform the division.

```
                                                   56.
  0.84)47.04          0.84)47.04.          0.84)47.04.
                                                42 0
                                                 5 04
                                                 5 04
                                                    0
```

Hence, the train requires exactly 56 gallons of diesel fuel to make the trip. Notice in this problem that when I shift the decimal point two places in both the divisor and dividend, in effect I am multiplying both by 100. Since I have done the same thing to both, this does not change the value of the expression.

Here is one more example you can show your youngster on dividing decimals; it illustrates how sometimes it is necessary to add zeros to both the dividend and the quotient in order to perform the division. Suppose, for example, that we want to divide 0.3077 by 8.5:

First shift the decimal one place to the right in both the divisor and dividend.

Next put the new decimal point in the quotient.

Then divide and add a zero in both the quotient and dividend.

$$8.5\overline{)0.3.077}$$

$$8.5\overline{)0.3.077}\,.$$

```
            .0362
8.5 )0.3.0770 ←
        2 55
         527
         510
         170
         170
           0
```

Just as there are many occasions to multiply decimals by 10, 100, and 1,000, there are also many situations when students will need to divide a decimal by one of these factors. Here again, the answer lies in knowing how to shift the decimal point. In such cases, all we need to do is move the decimal point one place to the left for each zero in the factor we are dividing by. Assume that we want to divide 75 by 10, 100, and 1,000:

$75 \div 10 = 7.5$ ←— Move the decimal point one place to the left.

$75 \div 100 = .75$ ←— Move the decimal point two places to the left.

$75 \div 1000 = .075$ ←— Move the decimal point three places to the left.

———— Notice also that you have to add one 0 before the 7.

The same approach applies to money. For example, to divide $7560. by 100:

$7560. ÷ 100 = $75.60 ⟵— Move the decimal point two places
                              to the left.

Rounding and Estimating

As with basic arithmetic, children need to know that rounding and estimating are useful techniques when working with decimals. If they do not have a calculator handy, they can round and estimate to get a basic idea of what an answer should look like. For example, if I want to buy 6 items in the grocery store that cost $1.95 each, I can get a good idea of how much money I will need by rounding $1.95 to $2.00 and multiplying by 6. This tells me that $12.00 should be enough to make my purchase (and maybe a little bit more for taxes!). And, as before, it is always helpful to do some mental arithmetic to determine what an answer should look like in a problem we are solving. We can compare this against our calculations to make sure our answer is reasonable.

Your child has already learned to round a number to a given place by merely looking at the next smaller digit. If this digit is equal to 5 or more, we increase the number in the given place by 1. If the next smaller digit is less than 5, then the number in the given place stays the same. All of the digits after the given place become 0, and thus do not appear in the answer. I will illustrate the approach in a division problem involving money. As you will see, not all problems come out so neatly as in the previous examples, and sometimes the digits in the quotient continue on and on.

Suppose I buy a package of snacks in the food store for $2.59. The package contains 12 snacks, and I want to figure out the cost per snack. To get the answer I need to divide $2.59 by 12:

Perform the division to one place beyond the place we want to round to.

Round the quotient to the nearest cent.

$$.215 \longrightarrow \$.22$$

```
    .215
12)2.590    The digits in this quotient
   2 4       continue indefinitely, but
    19        we do not need to go any
    12        further than thousandths.
    70
    60
    10
```

The snacks cost approximately $.22 each.

Summary

A knowledge of how to perform arithmetic operations with decimals is very useful. Children will use decimals in everyday situations like solving problems with money as well as making precise estimates of things in the physical world. While a calculator or a computer will enable them to make these computations much more quickly, a knowledge of how to work with numbers that are less than one is needed for an understanding of mathematics—especially in our next topic on fractions.

4

Fractions

So far we have reviewed basic arithmetic involving whole numbers and decimals. Very early in their lives children are introduced to the concept of fractions. This introduction occurs when they realize that it is possible to talk about parts of whole things, such as pieces of pie served at the dinner table. The use of fractions helps us understand how these separate pieces relate to each other, and also how they relate to the whole thing we are talking about. We often use fractions in our everyday lives, and need to know how to manipulate them in higher mathematics. We can use the methods of basic arithmetic to perform various calculations on fractions. Before discussing these, it will be useful for you to review some basic concepts of what mathematicians call number theory.

Some Basic Concepts

Least Common Multiple

The product of a given number, say 2, with any other number is a multiple of that given number. For example:

$$2 \times 0 = 0 \quad 2 \times 1 = 2 \quad 2 \times 2 = 4$$
$$2 \times 3 = 6 \quad 2 \times 4 = 8 \quad \ldots$$

The multiples of the number 2 are 0,2,4,6,8,10,12,14 . . .
The multiples of the number 3 are 0,3,6,9,12,15,18,21 . . .

The common multiples of the numbers 2 and 3 are 0,6,12 . . .

The least common multiple is just the smallest number (other than 0) that is common to both multiples. Thus, the least common multiple of the numbers 2 and 3 is 6.

Greatest Common Factor

We earlier described factors as the numbers multiplied together to yield a product. For example, the factors of the number 4 are:

$$1 \times 4 = 4 \qquad 2 \times 2 = 4 \qquad 4 \times 1 = 4$$

The factors of the number 8 are:

$$1 \times 8 = 8 \qquad 2 \times 4 = 8 \qquad 4 \times 2 = 8 \qquad 8 \times 1 = 8$$

The factors of 4 are: 1,2,4
The factors of 8 are: 1,2,4,8

The greatest common factor is the largest factor that is common to both numbers. Thus, the greatest common factor of 4 and 8 is 4.

Prime Factorization

A number is said to be *prime* if it has only two different factors—the number 1 and itself. For example, the numbers 2,3,5,7,11,13,17 . . . are prime because they can only be obtained by multiplying the number itself by 1:

$$1 \times 2 = 2 \qquad 1 \times 3 = 3 \qquad 1 \times 5 = 5 \qquad 1 \times 7 = 7 \quad \dots$$

On the other hand, *composite* numbers have more than two factors. Examples of composite numbers are 4,6,8,9,10,12,14, . . . because they have factors other than the number 1 and itself. For example,

$$1 \times 4 = 4 \qquad 1 \times 12 = 12 \qquad 2 \times 6 = 12$$
$$2 \times 2 = 4 \qquad \qquad \qquad \quad 3 \times 4 = 12$$

The factors of 4 are 1, 2, 4   The factors of 12 are 1, 2, 3, 4, 6, 12

The important point here is that a composite number can always be shown to be the product of prime numbers. We call this the *prime factorization* of a number. To illustrate this idea, you can show your child what mathematicians call a factor tree, which is nothing more than a pyramid that breaks composite numbers down into their prime numbers.

We can represent the number 24 using several different factor trees:

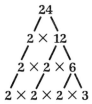 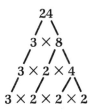 

Notice that not only can the number 24 be shown to be the product of prime numbers, in each case the prime factors are the same, regardless of the approach (factor tree) used.

Fractions

Parents should explain to children that we use fractions to represent portions of whole things or objects. For example, I could slice a pie into 8 equal pieces and represent each slice as a fraction equal to one-eighth. If I give 2 pieces of pie to my friends I have given them two-eighths, which is equal to one-quarter of the pie.

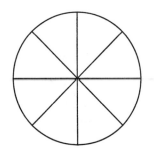

numerator → 1 ← each slice of pie
denominator → 8 ← total number of slices of pie

numerator → 2 ← slices I give to my friends
denominator → 8 ← total number of slices of pie

Emphasize that this illustrates an important concept. When two or more fractions refer to the same number of objects, they are called equivalent fractions. Such fractions can be obtained by multiplying both the numerator and denominator by the same number. This does not change the value of the fraction. In the above example,

$$\frac{1}{4} = \frac{1 \times 2}{4 \times 2} = \frac{2}{8}$$ Both the numerator and denominator of one-fourth have been multiplied by 2.

In fact, I could have divided both the numerator and denominator by the same number, and the fraction would still be equivalent.

$$\frac{2}{8} = \frac{2 \div 2}{8 \div 2} = \frac{1}{4}$$ Both the numerator and denominator of two-eighths have been divided by 2.

Students should know that this is an important technique for simplifying fractions. A fraction is said to be in its simplest form when both the numerator and denominator have no common factors other than 1. The quickest way to reduce a fraction to its simplest form is to divide both the numerator and denominator by their greatest common factor. To illustrate,

$$\frac{16}{20} = \frac{16 \div 2}{20 \div 2} = \frac{8 \div 2}{10 \div 2} = \frac{4}{5}$$ Both the numerator and denominator have been divided by 2, two separate times.

Alternatively, we could have divided the fraction by the greatest common factor of 16 and 20, which is 4.

$$\frac{16}{20} = \frac{16 \div 4}{20 \div 4} = \frac{4}{5}$$ Both the numerator and denominator have been divided by 4.

Mixed Numbers

Mixed numbers are numbers that have both a whole and fractional part. To illustrate the concept of mixed numbers to your child, you can return to the example involving pies. Except now suppose that we have 2 whole pies and three-fourths of another.

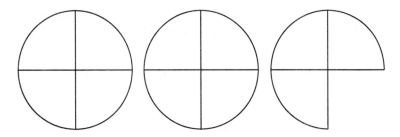

If we count up the number of fourths in all of the pies, the result is:

$$\frac{11}{4} = 2\frac{3}{4}$$ Where $\frac{11}{4}$ is an ordinary fraction and $2\frac{3}{4}$ is a mixed number.

While your child can see this relationship very easily from the diagram representing pies, explain that we need mathematical techniques to convert fractions to mixed numbers and mixed numbers to fractions. Suppose for example that we want to convert $\frac{11}{4}$ to a mixed number. We would proceed as follows:

First divide the denominator into the numerator.	Next write the quotient as a whole number.	Now write the remainder as a fraction, and add it to the whole number.
$\frac{11}{4} \rightarrow \begin{array}{r} 2 \\ 4\overline{)11} \\ \underline{8} \\ 3 \end{array}$	2	$2\frac{3}{4} \begin{array}{l} \leftarrow \text{remainder} \\ \leftarrow \text{divisor} \end{array}$

To convert a mixed number into an ordinary fraction, we merely reverse the procedure.

First multiply the whole number by the denominator.	Next add this product to the numerator.	Now write this sum over the denominator to get an ordinary fraction.
$2\dfrac{3}{4} \rightarrow 2 \times 4 = 8$	$8 + 3 = 11$	$\dfrac{11}{4}$

Adding Fractions

Students will soon learn that one of the things they frequently want to do is add fractions. This is a very simple matter when the fractions have the same denominator. In this case we simply add the numerators to get a new sum and divide it by the same denominator. For example, suppose I walk two-ninths of a mile to one friend's house and four-ninths of a mile to another friend's house. I might be interested in how far I walked to both friends' houses. This could be solved as follows:

$$\frac{2}{9} + \frac{4}{9} = \frac{2 + 4}{9} = \frac{6}{9} = \frac{2}{3}$$

Thus, I walked two-thirds of a mile altogether.

Explain to children that when the denominators of the two fractions are not the same, the calculation is only slightly more complex. In this case, **we** simply rewrite the fractions as equivalent fractions with the same denominator before we add them together. For example, if I walk two-ninths of a mile to one friend's house and one-sixth of a mile to another friend's house, I could find out how far I walked by making the following calculation:

$$\frac{2}{9} = \frac{2 \times 2}{9 \times 2} = \frac{4}{18}$$

$$+\frac{1}{6} = \frac{1 \times 3}{6 \times 3} = \frac{3}{18}$$

$$\frac{7}{18}$$

Here, I walked seven-eighteenths of a mile altogether.

Children should also know that sometimes we need to add fractions that are mixed numbers. When the denominators of the fractions in the mixed numbers are the same, the calculation is very straightforward. Suppose, for example, that I am a long-distance runner and I want to keep track of how far I run each day. On the first day I run three and one-half miles and on the second day I run four and one-half miles. I want to know how far I ran altogether over the two days. The calculation is as follows:

First add the fractions together.	Next add the whole numbers together.	Then rewrite the sum in its simplest form.

$$3\frac{1}{2}$$ $$+4\frac{1}{2}$$ $$\frac{2}{2}$$

$$3\frac{1}{2}$$ $$+4\frac{1}{2}$$ $$7\frac{2}{2}$$

$$7\frac{2}{2} = 8$$

I ran 8 miles over the two-day period.

When the mixed numbers do not have like fractions, explain that we first have to convert them into equivalent fractions before performing the addition. For example, if I ran three and one-half miles the first day and three and two-thirds miles the second day, I could figure out how much I had run during both days by making the following calculation:

First find fractions that have like denominators.	Next add the fractional and whole numbers.	Then write the sum in simplest form.

$$3\frac{1}{2} = 3\frac{3}{6}$$
$$+3\frac{2}{3} = 3\frac{4}{6}$$

$$3\frac{1}{2} = 3\frac{3}{6}$$
$$+3\frac{2}{3} = 3\frac{4}{6}$$
$$6\frac{7}{6}$$

$$6\frac{7}{6} = 6 + 1\frac{1}{6} = 7\frac{1}{6}$$

Thus, I ran seven and one-sixth miles altogether during both days.

Subtracting Fractions

We subtract fractions when we want to compare amounts, find out how much is left, or see how much more is needed. Subtracting fractions is very straightforward when both fractions have the same denominator. In this case, we simply subtract the numerators and divide the difference by the same denominator. For example, if I worked three-fourths of a day and my brother worked one-fourth of a day, I might want to know how much longer I worked than my brother. You can find the answer by the following calculation:

$$\frac{3}{4} - \frac{1}{4} = \frac{3-1}{4} = \frac{2}{4} = \frac{1}{2}$$

I worked one-half of a day longer than my brother.

Subtracting fractions with unlike denominators is similar to adding fractions with unlike denominators. We first have to write equivalent fractions with like denominators before we perform the calculation. As an example, if I worked three-fourths of a day and my brother worked one-fifth of a day, I could find out how much longer I worked than my brother by doing the following:

$$\frac{3}{4} = \frac{3 \times 5}{4 \times 5} = \frac{15}{20}$$
$$-\frac{1}{5} = \frac{1 \times 4}{5 \times 4} = \frac{4}{20}$$
$$\frac{11}{20}$$

This indicates that I worked eleven-twentieths of a day longer than my brother.

Once your child knows how to perform addition using mixed numbers, it is very easy to perform subtraction. Consider first the case where the fractional parts have the same denominators. Suppose it takes four and seven-eighths hours to fly an airplane to Los Angeles and two and five-eighths hours to fly to Chicago. We want to know how much longer it takes to fly to Los Angeles than to Chicago.

First subtract the fractional part.	Next subtract the whole numbers.	Then write the difference in its simplest form.
$$4\frac{7}{8}$$ $$-2\frac{5}{8}$$ $$\frac{2}{8}$$	$$4\frac{7}{8}$$ $$-2\frac{5}{8}$$ $$2\frac{2}{8}$$	$$2\frac{2}{8} = 2\frac{1}{4}$$

It takes two and one-fourth more hours to fly to Los Angeles than Chicago.

Now suppose that you want to explain how to subtract mixed numbers with fractions that have different denominators. As in addition, your child first needs to convert the fractions into equivalent fractions with like denominators before proceeding with the calculation. For example, suppose that it takes four and five-eighths hours to fly to San Diego and two and one-third hours to fly to Cleveland. How much longer does it take to fly to San Diego than to Cleveland?

First find equivalent fractions with like denominators.	Next subtract both the whole and fractional parts.	Then write the difference in simplest form.
$4\dfrac{5}{8} = 4\dfrac{15}{24}$ $-2\dfrac{1}{3} = 2\dfrac{8}{24}$	$4\dfrac{5}{8} = 4\dfrac{15}{24}$ $-2\dfrac{1}{3} = 2\dfrac{8}{24}$ $\overline{2\dfrac{7}{24}}$	$2\dfrac{7}{24}$ is in simplest form.

It takes two and seven twenty-fourths more hours to fly to San Diego than to Cleveland.

In both of these examples involving mixed numbers, your child has been able to subtract the fractional parts without much difficulty. In cases where she cannot subtract the fractional parts directly, she needs to rename the mixed numbers before performing the calculation. For example, suppose it takes one and three-quarter hours to fly to New York and two and one-third hours to fly to New Orleans. How much longer does it take to fly to New Orleans than to New York?

First find fractions with like denominators.	Next compare fractions and rename them, if necessary.	Then perform the subtraction.
$2\dfrac{1}{3} = 2\dfrac{4}{12}$ $-1\dfrac{3}{4} = 1\dfrac{9}{12}$	$\dfrac{9}{12} > \dfrac{4}{12}$, so $2\dfrac{4}{12} = 1 + 1\dfrac{4}{12} = 1\dfrac{16}{12}$	$1\dfrac{16}{12}$ $-1\dfrac{9}{12}$ $\overline{\dfrac{7}{12}}$

It takes seven-twelfths of an hour longer to fly to New Orleans than to New York.

Multiplying Fractions

Students will encounter many occasions where it is necessary to multiply fractions together to solve a problem. These typically occur when it is necessary to find an amount that is a fraction of something that is already a fraction itself. If this sounds confusing to your child, let me illustrate it with an example. Suppose I purchase three-fourths of a yard of material from the fabric store. Now suppose that I need to use eight-ninths of the material to make pillow coverings. I can find out how much material I have used altogether by multiplying the fractions together.

First multiply the numerators together.	Next multiply the denominators together.	Then write the product in simplest form.
$\dfrac{8}{9} \times \dfrac{3}{4} = \dfrac{24}{}$	$\dfrac{8}{9} \times \dfrac{3}{4} = \dfrac{24}{36}$	$\dfrac{24}{36} = \dfrac{2}{3}$

I used two-thirds of a yard of material to make the pillow coverings.

Actually, you can explain to your youngster that there is a much simpler, shorter way to solve this problem. I could have divided both numerators and denominators by common factors before carrying out the rest of the calculation. To illustrate, in the above example, 4 is a common factor of 4 and 8, so I can divide both 4 and 8 by 4 before multiplying numerators and denominators to get the answer. Notice that 3 is a common factor of 3 and 9, so I can also divide both 3 and 9 by 3 before multiplying numerators and denominators together.

$$\frac{\overset{2}{\cancel{8}}}{\underset{3}{\cancel{9}}} \times \frac{\overset{1}{\cancel{3}}}{\underset{1}{\cancel{4}}} = \frac{2 \times 1}{3 \times 1} = \frac{2}{3}$$

Emphasize that you get the same answer with the short approach and use much smaller numbers in the process. This can be a significant savings of work in longer, more complicated problems.

Sometimes it is necessary to multiply fractions by whole numbers to solve a problem. This should not present any difficulty to children, as soon as they realize that a whole number is nothing more than a fraction with a denominator of 1. To illustrate, in the above example we found that it takes two-thirds of a yard of material to make pillow coverings. Suppose that my design for pillow coverings is so successful that I decide to go into business for myself and sell them commercially. As a start, I assume that I will need six times as many pillow coverings on my shelf at the store. How much material is needed to make the pillow coverings?

First write the whole number as a fraction.	Next divide by any common factors.	Then multiply the fractions together.	Finally, write the product in simplest form.
$\frac{2}{3} \times \frac{6}{1}$	$\frac{2}{\overset{}{\underset{1}{3}}} \times \frac{\overset{2}{6}}{1}$	$\frac{2 \times 2}{1 \times 1} = \frac{4}{1}$	$\frac{4}{1} = 4$

Thus, I need 4 yards of material to make six times as many pillow coverings.

If students are required to multiply fractions by mixed numbers, or mixed numbers by mixed numbers, they only need to convert them into ordinary fractions first before making similar calculations. Suppose in the above example that I want to get six and one-half times as much material to make my pillow coverings because I am afraid that I may make some mistakes in the process. Remembering that it takes two-thirds of a yard of material for one set of pillow coverings, I would:

Convert the mixed number into an ordinary fraction.	Next multiply the fractions together.	Then write the product in its simplest form.
$6\frac{1}{2} = \frac{13}{2}$	$\frac{\overset{1}{2}}{3} \times \frac{13}{\underset{1}{2}} = \frac{13}{3}$	$\frac{13}{3} = 4\frac{1}{3}$

I would need four and one-third yards of material for my pillow coverings.

Dividing Fractions

Children will also encounter many occasions when they need to divide fractions to solve problems. Actually, division of fractions is no more difficult than multiplication of fractions, once they realize that they first have to find the *reciprocal* of the fraction they are dividing by; then everything else is the same. Reciprocals are nothing more than numbers whose product is 1. For example, to find the reciprocal of two-thirds we observe the following:

$\frac{2}{3} \times \frac{3}{2} = 1$ Therefore, three-halves is the reciprocal of two-thirds. All we have done is to flip the fraction upside down.

Division problems involving fractions are of the following type. Suppose I want to make several batches of cookies for a picnic outing. If I have five pounds of sugar and it takes five-eighths of a pound of sugar to make each batch, how many batches of cookies can I make? To solve this problem we need to divide five by five-eighths.

First write the whole number as a fraction.	Next multiply by the reciprocal of the divisor.	Then write the product in its simplest form.
$5 \div \frac{5}{8} = \frac{5}{1} \div \frac{5}{8}$	$\frac{\overset{1}{\cancel{5}}}{1} \times \frac{8}{\underset{1}{\cancel{5}}} = \frac{8}{1}$	$\frac{8}{1} = 8$

I can make eight batches of cookies with five pounds of sugar.

If your child is asked to divide a mixed number by a fraction, all he needs to do is first convert the mixed number into an ordinary fraction and then everything else proceeds just as before. Suppose, as in the above example, that it still takes five-eighths of a pound of sugar to make a batch of cookies, but now I have eight and one-half pounds of sugar and want to know how many batches of cookies I can make. The calculation would be as follows:

First convert the mixed number into an ordinary fraction.	Next multiply by the reciprocal of the fraction that is the divisor.	Then write the product in its simplest form.
$8\frac{1}{2} \div \frac{5}{8} = \frac{17}{2} \div \frac{5}{8}$	$\frac{17}{\underset{1}{2}} \times \frac{\overset{4}{8}}{5} = \frac{68}{5}$	$\frac{68}{5} = 13\frac{3}{5}$

Thus, with eight and one-half pounds of sugar I can make thirteen and three-fifths batches of cookies.

The examples in this section make it clear that whether we are dividing whole numbers, mixed numbers, or even fractions by fractions the approach is the same. Find the reciprocal of the divisor and then proceed as in multiplication.

Summary

I have spent much time on arithmetical operations involving fractions for two major reasons. The first is that we often need to make calculations involving fractions as part of our everyday lives. The second and more important reason—at least for the purpose of this book—is that an ability to carry out operations involving fractions is necessary if students are to master the subject of algebra. Many people have trouble with algebra simply because they never learned the proper way to work with fractions. Your child should now have enough background on this subject to master what lies ahead of us.

5

Ratios, Proportions, and Percents

Both children and adults need a knowledge of ratios, proportions, and percents in order to solve many practical, everyday problems. These new concepts are useful for comparing two related numbers or comparing one number to a hundred. In fact, your child will usually see these concepts referred to in written material about numbers because they are so useful for comparing and summarizing information. Now that your child has a basic understanding of decimals and fractions, it is relatively easy to extend this knowledge to an understanding of ratios, proportions, and percents. In fact, he or she will see that all of these concepts are closely related, and very often one can be derived from another. Before we discuss ratios, proportions, and percents, it will be useful to review some basics about solving an equation with an unknown value.

Equations

An equation is just an expression that says the quantities to the left of the equal sign equal the quantities to the right of the equal sign. For example, if I write the following equation with an unknown value, say n, then to solve the equation I need to find the value of n that makes the statement true:

$$5 + n = 9$$

Just looking at this equation, I know that the value of n is 4, because this is the only value that makes the statement true.

Explain to children that they need to find a more systematic way of solving for n, because not all equations are so obvious. The goal is to end up with an expression in which n is the only value to the left of the equal sign, and all other values are to the right. This, in effect, tells us what n is equal to. In order to move the other numbers around and keep the value of the equation the same, the principal rule to emphasize is that whatever you do to one side of the equation you must also do to the other side. For example, in the above example, if I subtract 5 from each side of the equation then I have not really changed anything. But this enables me to solve for the value of n:

$$(5 + n) - 5 = 9 - 5$$
$$\cancel{5} + n - \cancel{5} = 9 - 5$$
$$n = 4$$

As your child performs the calculations, instruct him to do the ones inside the parentheses first, and then proceed from left to right. I will have much more to say on the proper order of operations in a later chapter on algebra.

As another example, suppose your child is trying to solve the value of n in the equation $n - 7 = 6$. He can see that by adding 7 to each side of the equation he can end up with n on the left and everything else on the right:

$$(n - 7) + 7 = 6 + 7$$
$$n - \cancel{7} + \cancel{7} = 13$$
$$n = 13$$

He would use the same type of approach to solve for n if he was faced with an equation that involves a multiplication of n by a number. For example, to solve the equation $n \times 4 = 28$, he would divide each side of the equation by 4:

$$(n \times 4) \div 4 = 28 \div 4$$

$$n \times \overset{1}{\cancel{4}} \times \frac{1}{\underset{1}{\cancel{4}}} = 7$$

$$n = 7$$

Your child should now be able to see that if n is divided by some number on the left of the equation, he can solve for n by multiplying both sides of the equation by the same number. As an example, to solve $n \div 6 = 6$, he would proceed as follows:

$$(n \div 6) \times 6 = 6 \times 6$$

$$n \times \frac{1}{\underset{1}{\cancel{6}}} \times \overset{1}{\cancel{6}} = 36$$

$$n = 36$$

I will also have a lot more to say about solving for unknowns in the later chapter on algebra but, for now, this should be sufficient to master the material at hand.

Ratios

A ratio is used to compare two related numbers. To illustrate the concept of a ratio to children, you can use an example from baseball. Suppose that a certain player gets 7 hits for 20 times at bat. The ratio of hits to the total number of times at bat can be expressed as:

$$\frac{7}{20} \quad \text{or} \quad 7 \text{ to } 20 \quad \text{or} \quad 7{:}20$$

Explain to your children that they can also think of this ratio as a rate. An expression is a rate when two numbers are compared by words such as *per*, *for*, or *each*. For example, we would be referring to a rate if we said:

> The batter gets 7 hits *per* 20 times at bat.
> The batter gets 7 hits *for* every 20 times at bat.
> The batter gets 7 hits *each* 20 times at bat.

Suppose I want to know how many hits this player would get in 40 times at bat, if he continues to hit at the same rate. I can use equal ratios to solve this problem. I am trying to find some unknown number of hits—call this value n—for 40 times at bat. Here is how to set it up:

Set up equal ratios.	Find equivalent fractions.	Solve the problem.
hits $\dfrac{7}{20} = \dfrac{n}{40}$ times at bat	Looking at the denominator, we see that $20 \times 2 = 40$.	$\dfrac{7}{20} = \dfrac{7 \times 2}{20 \times 2} = \dfrac{14}{40}$

We expect the player to have 14 hits for 40 times at bat, if he continues to hit at the same rate. Notice that to solve the problem, all we have done is to multiply the numerator by the same factor (2) as in the denominator.

Proportions

Students should also know that when we have equal ratios, as in the above example, we say that they are a proportion. We can tell if two ratios are a proportion if we get the same result when we cross-multiply their numerators and denominators. We can illustrate this using the above example:

hits	$7 \diagdown 14$	$7 \times 40 = 280$	Hence, the two ratios
times at bat	$20 \diagup 40$	$20 \times 14 = 280$	are a proportion.

Some books may express the same relationship by saying that two or more ratios are *proportional* to each other.

Actually, we could have used the same approach of cross-multiplying numerators and denominators to solve for the missing value of n in the above example.

$$\frac{n}{40} \diagdown \frac{7}{20}$$

$$n \times 20 = 7 \times 40$$
$$n \times 20 \div 20 = 7 \times 40 \div 20$$
$$n = 280 \div 20$$
$$n = 14$$

Note that after I cross-multiply the numerators and denominators together, I have an equation in which I need to solve for the value of n. I can divide both the left and right sides of the equation by 20, which does not change the value of the expression. Then I can solve for n.

This approach also shows that I expect the batter to have 14 hits out of 40 times at bat.

Percents

A percent is essentially a ratio that compares some number to a hundred. In the above example, your youngster might want to know how many hits we expect the player to get for 100 times at bat, if he continues to hit at the same rate. To solve this problem, we could use an approach similar to the one shown above:

First find an equivalent fraction for the ratio that has a denominator equal to 100.

$$\frac{7}{20} = \frac{7 \times 5}{20 \times 5} = \frac{35}{100}$$

When a fraction has a denominator of 100, we can write its numerator as a percent.

$$\frac{35}{100} = 35\%$$ where % refers to percent.

Actually, we could have converted the *original* ratio into a percent by dividing its denominator into its numerator. This yields a decimal value, which can be multiplied by 100 to equal a percent. Emphasize to your children that this shows that any ratio or fraction can be converted into a decimal by dividing its denominator into its numerator. To illustrate:

First divide the denominator of the ratio into its numerator.

Then multiply the decimal value by 100 to express it as a percent.

$$\begin{array}{r} .350 \\ 20\overline{)7.000} \\ \underline{6\ 0} \\ 1\ 00 \\ \underline{1\ 00} \\ 0 \\ \underline{0} \end{array}$$

$.350 \times 100 = 35.0\%$

In the above division I have calculated the decimal to thousandths because this is the way batting averages are normally expressed. Thus, when we say that a player is batting .350, we mean that he gets a hit 35 out of 100—or 35 percent—of his times at bat.

We can turn the problem around slightly by asking how many hits the player will get for 260 times at bat, if he continues to maintain the same batting average. To find the answer to this question, we could change the percent back to either a fraction or decimal, and then multiply it by the total number of times at bat. To illustrate:

Change the percent to a fraction.

And then multiply it by the total.

$$35\% = \frac{35}{100} = \frac{7}{20}$$

$$\frac{7}{\underset{1}{\cancel{20}}} \times \overset{13}{\cancel{260}} = 7 \times 13 = 91$$

This says that the batter should get 91 hits for 260 times at bat. Alternatively, we could use the following approach:

Change the percent to a decimal.	And then multiply it by the total.

$$35\% = 0.35$$

$$
\begin{array}{r}
260 \\
\times\ .35 \\
\hline
13\ 00 \\
78\ 0 \\
\hline
91.00
\end{array}
$$

This yields the same answer: 91 hits for 260 times at bat.

It is important for students to become comfortable at working with percents, because problems can be stated in a variety of ways. For example, if another player gets 65 hits out of 260 times at bat, we can calculate the percent of hits he gets in the following way:

First write an equation.	Then solve the equation.	Convert to percent.

$$
\begin{aligned}
n \times 260 &= 65 \\
(n \times 260) \div 260 &= 65 \div 260 \\
n &= 65 \div 260
\end{aligned}
$$

$$
\begin{array}{r}
.250 \\
260\overline{)65.000} \\
52\ 0 \\
\hline
13\ 00 \\
13\ 00 \\
\hline
0
\end{array}
$$

$$.250 \times 100 = 25\%$$

This player gets a hit 25% of the time.

Summary

We have examined a number of problems involving ratios, proportions, and percents, as applied to the example of base-ball batting averages. These same concepts are useful for a huge number of similar applications. For example, explain to your children that they can calculate the percent of money (interest) they are earning on their savings account, the percent of problems they solved correctly on their math test, the ratio of rainy days to clear days last year, and just about anything else they can think of that involves numbers. It is important for them to become familiar with these concepts because they will encounter them almost every day for the rest of their lives. (Just think—for most things that we buy at a store, we are probably paying a tax that is some percentage of the purchase price!)

6

Weights and Measures

We now move from the world of arithmetic operations to the measurement of things in the physical world. The concepts we will be discussing include time, temperature, length, capacity, and weight (and mass). Many children are familiar with our customary units of measure but they have more difficulty when working with metric measures. A knowledge of the metric system is important because it is the standard of measurement for scientific work and the basic system of measurement used by most of the world. Learning the metric system is even more important because one day it will be the basic system of measurement in the United States as well. This transition is apparent not only from the appearance of metric measures in our everyday lives, but also from the emphasis the metric system is getting in school curricula from the earliest years. We will review our customary measures first and then discuss metric measures.

Customary Units of Measure

Our customary units of measure for *time* are well known to children from their earliest years. They include seconds (s), minutes (min), hours (h), days (d), weeks (wk), months (mo), years (y), centuries (c), and millennia (m). The following table shows equivalent measures of time:

60 seconds = 1 minute	52 weeks = 1 year
60 minutes = 1 hour	12 months = 1 year
24 hours = 1 day	100 years = 1 century
7 days = 1 week	1000 years = 1 millennium
365 days = 1 year	

You can review some examples that show your youngster how to make conversions between these units of time and perform arithmetic with them. To convert larger units to smaller units, you should multiply:

Convert hours to minutes.

$$6 \text{ h} \quad 25 \text{ min} \quad = \text{ ? min}$$
$$(6 \times 60) + 25 = 385$$
$$6 \text{ h} \quad 25 \text{ min} \quad = 385 \text{ min}$$

Convert years to months.

$$3 \text{ y} \quad 7 \text{ mo} \quad = \text{ ? mo}$$
$$(3 \times 12) + 7 = 43$$
$$3 \text{ y} \quad 7 \text{ mo} \quad = 43 \text{ mo}$$

To convert smaller units to larger units, you should divide:

Convert seconds to minutes.

$$390 \text{ s} \quad = \text{ ? min}$$
$$(390 \div 60) = 6\frac{1}{2}$$
$$390 \text{ s} \quad = 6\frac{1}{2} \text{ min}$$

Convert years to centuries.

$$575 \text{ y} \quad = \text{ ? c}$$
$$(575 \div 100) = 5\frac{3}{4}$$
$$575 \text{ y} \quad = 5\frac{3}{4} \text{ c}$$

To perform addition and subtraction with customary units of time:

Addition.

$$
\begin{array}{ll}
& 4 \text{ h} \quad 45 \text{ min} \\
+ & 5 \text{ h} \quad 25 \text{ min} \\
\hline
& 9 \text{ h} \quad 70 \text{ min} \\
= & 10 \text{ h} \quad 10 \text{ min}
\end{array}
\left\{
\begin{array}{l}
\text{Rename} \\
70 \text{ min} \\
\text{as} \\
1 \text{ h} \quad 10 \text{ min}
\end{array}
\right.
$$

Subtraction.

$$
\begin{array}{lll}
& 26 \text{ min} & 78 \text{ s} \\
& \cancel{27} \text{ min} & \cancel{18} \text{ s} \\
- & 13 \text{ min} & 56 \text{ s} \\
\hline
& 13 \text{ min} & 22 \text{ s}
\end{array}
\left\{
\begin{array}{l}
\text{Rename} \\
27 \text{ min} \quad 18 \text{ s} \\
\text{as} \\
26 \text{ min} \quad 78 \text{ s}
\end{array}
\right.
$$

Our customary units of measure for *temperature* are the Fahrenheit and Celsius scales. The former is measured in degrees Fahrenheit (°F), and the latter is measured in degrees Celsius (°C). As reference points, on the Fahrenheit scale water freezes at 32°F and boils at 212°F, while on the Celsius scale water freezes at 0°C and boils at 100°C. The Celsius scale, which is obviously more compressed, is used for most scientific work, while the Fahrenheit scale is used for most practical applications. Although Celsius is a metric scale, I will present both scales in this section to show how to make conversions between them:

From Fahrenheit to Celsius.	From Celsius to Fahrenheit.
$C = \dfrac{5}{9} \times (F - 32)$	$F = \dfrac{9}{5} \times C + 32$

Here are a few examples illustrating these conversions. To help your child solve these, show how to substitute the values into the above formulae:

Convert 59° Fahrenheit to Celsius.

$$C = \frac{5}{9} \times (59 - 32)$$

$$C = \frac{5}{\overset{}{\underset{1}{9}}} \times \overset{3}{27}$$

$$C = 15°$$

Convert 30° Celsius to Fahrenheit.

$$F = \frac{9}{\underset{1}{5}} \times \overset{6}{30} + 32$$

$$F = 54 + 32$$

$$F = 86°$$

Our customary units of measure for *length* are inches (in.), feet (ft), yards (yd), and miles (mi). Here is a useful table that relates these measures to each other:

---

12 inches = 1 foot	3 feet = 1 yard	5,280 feet = 1 mile
which tells us that:	36 inches = 1 yard	1,760 yards = 1 mile

It will be useful to review some examples with children to show them how to make conversions between these units of measure and perform arithmetic with them. For example, if you want to convert larger units to smaller units, you should multiply:

Convert feet to inches.	Convert yards to feet.
6 ft 3 in. = ? in.	13 yd 2 ft = ? ft
(6 × 12) + 3 = 75	(13 × 3) + 2 = 41
6 ft 3 in. = 75 in.	13 yd 2 ft = 41 ft

If you want to convert smaller units to larger units, you should divide:

Convert feet to yards.

$$83 \text{ ft} = ? \text{ yd.}$$
$$(83 \div 3) = 27\frac{2}{3}$$
$$83 \text{ ft} = 27\frac{2}{3} \text{ yd}$$

Convert yards to miles.

$$9,240 \text{ yd} = ? \text{ mi}$$
$$(9,240 \div 1,760) = 5\frac{1}{4}$$
$$9,240 \text{ yd} = 5\frac{1}{4} \text{ mi}$$

You can also perform addition and subtraction with customary units of length:

Addition.

$$\begin{array}{ll} 13 \text{ ft} & 8 \text{ in.} \\ + 6 \text{ ft} & 5 \text{ in.} \\ \hline 19 \text{ ft} & 13 \text{ in.} \\ = 20 \text{ ft} & 1 \text{ in.} \end{array} \left\{ \begin{array}{l} \text{Rename} \\ \text{13 in.} \\ \text{as} \\ \text{1 ft   1 in.} \end{array} \right.$$

Subtraction.

$$\begin{array}{ll} 4 \text{ mi} & 2,036 \text{ yd} \\ \cancel{5} \text{ mi} & \cancel{276} \text{ yd} \\ - 3 \text{ mi} & 1,025 \text{ yd} \\ \hline 1 \text{ mi} & 1,011 \text{ yd} \end{array} \left\{ \begin{array}{l} \text{Rename} \\ \text{5 mi   276 yd} \\ \text{as} \\ \text{4 mi   2,036 yd} \end{array} \right.$$

Our customary units of measure for *capacity* are fluid ounces (fl oz), cups (c), pints (pt), quarts (qt), and gallons (gal). The following table relates these measures to each other:

8 fluid ounces = 1 cup	2 pints = 1 quart
2 cups = 1 pint	4 quarts = 1 gallon

Your child will benefit by looking at some examples that show how to make conversions and perform arithmetic with these units of measure. For example, to convert larger units to smaller units, you should multiply:

Convert cups to fluid ounces.   Convert gallons to quarts.

14 c   3 fl oz = ? fl oz   6 gal   2 qt   = ? qt
(14 × 8) + 3 = 115   (6 × 4) + 2 = 26
14 c   3 fl oz = 115 fl oz   6 gal   2 qt   = 26 qt

To convert smaller units to larger units, you should divide:

Convert cups to pints.   Convert quarts to gallons.

26 c   = ? pt   32 qt   = ? qal
(26 ÷ 2) = 13   (32 ÷ 4) = 8
26 c   = 13 pt   32 qt   = 8 gal

And, as before, we can perform addition and subtraction with our customary units of capacity. Here are some examples:

Addition.   Subtraction.

  6 c   7 fl oz   8 gal   5 qt ⎧ Rename
+ 4 c   6 fl oz ⎧ Rename   9 gal   1 qt ⎨ 9 gal   1 qt
─────────────   ⎪ 13 fl oz   − 4 gal   3 qt ⎪   as
 10 c   13 fl oz ⎨   as   ───────────── ⎩ 8 gal   5 qt
=11 c   5 fl oz ⎪ 1 c   5 fl oz   4 gal   2 qt
                 ⎩

Our customary units of measure for *weight* are ounces (oz), pounds (lb), and tons (T). The relationship between these measures is shown in the following table.

16 ounces = 1 pound	2,000 pounds = 1 ton

Here are a few examples you can use to show your child how to make conversions and perform arithmetic with these units of measure. To convert larger units to smaller units you should multiply:

Convert pounds to ounces.

5 lb	4 oz	= ? oz
(5 × 16) + 4		= 84
5 lb	4 oz	= 84 oz

Convert tons to pounds.

4 T	1,150 lb	= ? lb
(4 × 2,000) + 1,150		= 9,150
4 T	1,150 lb	= 9,150 lb

To convert smaller units to larger units, you should divide:

Convert ounces to pounds.

100 oz	= ? lb
(100 ÷ 16)	= $6\frac{1}{4}$
100 oz	= $6\frac{1}{4}$ lb

Convert pounds to tons.

7,500 lb	= ? T
(7,500 ÷ 2,000)	= $3\frac{3}{4}$
7,500 lb	= $3\frac{3}{4}$ T

Finally, to illustrate addition and subtraction to your children with these customary units of weight:

Addition.

$$\begin{array}{rr} 14\text{ lb} & 13\text{ oz} \\ +\ 5\text{ lb} & 7\text{ oz} \\ \hline 19\text{ lb} & 20\text{ oz} \\ =20\text{ lb} & 4\text{ oz} \end{array}$$

$\left\{\begin{array}{l} \text{Rename} \\ 20\text{ oz} \\ \text{as} \\ 1\text{ lb}\quad 4\text{ oz} \end{array}\right.$

Subtraction.

$$\begin{array}{rr} 6\text{ T} & 2,675\text{ lb} \\ 7\text{ T} & \cancel{675}\text{ lb} \\ -3\text{ T} & 1,275\text{ lb} \\ \hline 3\text{ T} & 1,400\text{ lb} \end{array}$$

$\left\{\begin{array}{l} \text{Rename} \\ 7\text{ T}\quad 675\text{ lb} \\ \text{as} \\ 6\text{ T}\quad 2,675\text{ lb} \end{array}\right.$

Metric Units of Measure

Both children and adults feel very comfortable with our customary units of measure because they use them every day. These measures become second nature to us. The metric system seems strange—even foreign!—to us because we do not use it often and the labels seem complex and confusing. Actually, the metric system is very logical and easy to learn once we realize that the various measures along the metric scale differ from each other by factors of ten.

We will start off with the basic metric measure of length, which is the *meter*. The meter is a little more than one yard long. This is easy enough to understand, but the difficulty usually comes when trying to understand and remember the various measures related to the meter. Ranging from smallest to largest, they are the millimeter, centimeter, decimeter, meter, dekameter, hectometer, and kilometer. The relationship between these measures is as follows:

$$10 \text{ millimeters (mm)} = 1 \text{ centimeter (cm)}$$
$$10 \text{ centimeters (cm)} = 1 \text{ decimeter (dm)}$$
$$10 \text{ decimeters (dm)} = 1 \text{ meter (m)}$$
$$10 \text{ meters (m)} = 1 \text{ dekameter (dam)}$$
$$10 \text{ dekameters (dam)} = 1 \text{ hectometer (hm)}$$
$$10 \text{ hectometers (hm)} = 1 \text{ kilometer (km)}$$

Notice that going from the smallest to the largest measure, each differs from the previous one by a factor of ten, as stated above.

In order to give students a feel for the distances involved in these measures, consider the following scale for the smaller measures:

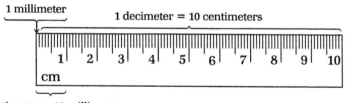

The following chart will help children see the relationship between each of these measures and the meter, and show them how to make conversions between them. A good way to remember the order of these measures is the popular childhood saying: <u>K</u>ing <u>H</u>enry <u>D</u>ied <u>M</u>onday <u>D</u>rinking <u>C</u>hocolate <u>M</u>ilk, where the first letter of each word in the saying refers to the first letter of metric lengths from largest (kilometer) to smallest (millimeter).

<u>K</u>ing	<u>H</u>enry	<u>D</u>ied	<u>M</u>onday	<u>D</u>rinking	<u>C</u>hocolate	<u>M</u>ilk
km	hm	dam	m	dm	cm	mm
kilometer	hectometer	dekameter	meter	decimeter	centimeter	millimeter
1km = 1000m	1hm = 100m	1dam = 10m		10dm = 1m	100cm = 1m	1000mm = 1m

From this scale, we can see that 1 km = 1,000 m, 1 hm = 100 m, and so on. The general rule is that to convert from larger units to smaller units you should multiply. Here are some examples you can show your youngster:

Convert kilometers to meters.

1.987 km = ? m
1.987 × 1,000 = 1987
1.987 km = 1987 m

{ To multiply by 1,000, shift decimal 3 to the right.

Convert meters to centimeters.

1.45 m = ? cm
1.45 × 100 = 145
1.45 m = 145 cm

{ To multiply by 100, shift decimal 2 to the right.

To convert from smaller units to larger units, you should divide:

Convert meters to hectometers.

65.2 m = ? hm
65.2 ÷ 100 = .652
65.2 m = .652 hm

{ To divide by 100, shift decimal 2 to the left.

Convert millimeters to meters.

$$
\begin{array}{ll}
\text{397 mm} & = \text{? m} \\
\text{397} \div \text{1,000} & = .397 \\
\text{397 mm} & = .397 \text{ m}
\end{array}
\quad
\left\{
\begin{array}{l}
\text{To divide by} \\
\text{1,000, shift} \\
\text{decimal 3} \\
\text{to the left.}
\end{array}
\right.
$$

Children should also know that they can convert to units not involving meters, as long as they move the decimal point by the right number of places. To realize this, consider the following examples.

Convert hectometers to decimeters.

$$
\begin{array}{ll}
.391 \text{ hm} & = \text{? dm} \\
.391 \times \text{1,000} & = 391 \\
.391 \text{ hm} & = 391 \text{ dm}
\end{array}
\quad
\left\{
\begin{array}{l}
\text{To multiply by} \\
\text{1,000, shift} \\
\text{decimal 3} \\
\text{to the right.}
\end{array}
\right.
$$

Convert millimeters to decimeters.

$$
\begin{array}{ll}
26.7 \text{ mm} & = \text{? dm} \\
26.7 \div 100 & = .267 \\
26.7 \text{ mm} & = .267 \text{ dm}
\end{array}
\quad
\left\{
\begin{array}{l}
\text{To divide by} \\
\text{100, shift} \\
\text{decimal 2} \\
\text{to the left.}
\end{array}
\right.
$$

The metric unit of *capacity* is the liter. A liter is a little more than a quart. The various measures related to the liter, ranging from the smallest to the largest, are the milliliter, centiliter, deciliter, liter, dekaliter, hectoliter, and kiloliter. (Notice that the prefixes for all of the other measures are the same as the ones we encountered for length, which makes them easy to remember.) The relationship between these measures is as follows:

$$
\begin{array}{rcl}
\text{10 milliliters (ml)} & = & \text{1 centiliter (cl)} \\
\text{10 centiliters (cl)} & = & \text{1 deciliter (dl)} \\
\text{10 deciliters (dl)} & = & \text{1 liter (l)} \\
\text{10 liters (l)} & = & \text{1 dekaliter (dal)} \\
\text{10 dekaliters (dal)} & = & \text{1 hectoliter (hl)} \\
\text{10 hectoliters (hl)} & = & \text{1 kiloliter (kl)}
\end{array}
$$

Notice that going from the smallest to the largest measure, each differs from the previous one by a factor of ten, just as before.

The following chart will help children to see the relationship between each of these measures and the liter, and show them how to make conversions between them. We will change the popular childhood saying to: King Henry Died Later Drinking Chocolate Milk, where the first letter of each word in the saying refers to the first letter of metric capacity from largest (kiloliter) to smallest (milliliter).

King	Henry	Died	Later	Drinking	Chocolate	Milk
kl	hl	dal	l	dl	cl	ml
kiloliter	hectoliter	dekaliter	liter	deciliter	centiliter	milliliter
1 kl = 1000 l	1 hl = 100 l	1 dal = 10 l		10 dl = 1 l	100 cl = 1 l	1000 ml = 1 l

From this scale, we can see that 1 kl = 1,000 l, 1 hl = 100 l, and so on. As before, the general rule is that to convert from larger units to smaller units you should multiply. Here are some examples you can show to your child:

Convert kiloliters to liters.

$$6.814 \text{ kl} \qquad = ? \text{ l}$$
$$6.814 \times 1,000 = 6814$$
$$6.814 \text{ kl} \qquad = 6814 \text{ l}$$

To multiply by 1,000, shift decimal 3 to the right.

Convert liters to centiliters.

$$3.21 \text{ l} \qquad = ? \text{ cl}$$
$$3.21 \times 100 = 321$$
$$3.21 \text{ l} \qquad = 321 \text{ cl}$$

To multiply by 100, shift decimal 2 to the right.

To convert from smaller units to larger units, you should divide:

Convert liters to hectoliters.

$$
\begin{array}{ll}
34.8\ \text{l} & = \text{? hl} \\
34.8\ \div\ 100 & = .348 \\
34.8\ \text{l} & = .348\ \text{hl}
\end{array}
\left\{
\begin{array}{l}
\text{To divide by} \\
\text{100, shift} \\
\text{decimal 2} \\
\text{to the left.}
\end{array}
\right.
$$

Convert milliliters to liters.

$$
\begin{array}{ll}
749\ \text{ml} & = \text{? l} \\
749\ \div\ 1{,}000 & = .749 \\
749\ \text{ml} & = .749\ \text{l}
\end{array}
\left\{
\begin{array}{l}
\text{To divide by} \\
\text{1,000, shift} \\
\text{decimal 3} \\
\text{to the left.}
\end{array}
\right.
$$

Make sure children also know that they can convert to units not involving liters, as long as they move the decimal point by the right number of places. This is illustrated in the following examples:

Convert hectoliters to deciliters.

$$
\begin{array}{ll}
.193\ \text{hl} & = \text{? dl} \\
.193\ \times\ 1{,}000 & = 193 \\
.193\ \text{hl} & = 193\ \text{dl}
\end{array}
\left\{
\begin{array}{l}
\text{To multiply by} \\
\text{1,000, shift} \\
\text{decimal 3} \\
\text{to the right.}
\end{array}
\right.
$$

Convert milliliters to deciliters.

$$
\begin{array}{ll}
45.9\ \text{ml} & = \text{? dl} \\
45.9\ \div\ 100 & = .459 \\
45.9\ \text{ml} & = .459\ \text{dl}
\end{array}
\left\{
\begin{array}{l}
\text{To divide by} \\
\text{100, shift} \\
\text{decimal 2} \\
\text{to the left.}
\end{array}
\right.
$$

The final metric unit we will consider is that of mass. (We will not cover the metric units of area and volume, because these concepts will not be introduced until the next chapter on geometry.) The metric unit of *mass* is the gram. A gram is only a fraction of an ounce (.035 ounce). The various measures related to the gram, ranging from the smallest to the largest, are the milligram, centigram, decigram, gram, dekagram, hectogram, and kilogram. (For symmetry, I will not discuss the metric ton, which equals 1,000,000 grams.) As before, the prefixes for all of the other measures are the same as the ones we encountered for length and capacity, which makes them easy to remember. The relationship between these measures is as follows:

$$10 \text{ milligrams (mg)} = 1 \text{ centigram (cg)}$$
$$10 \text{ centigrams (cg)} = 1 \text{ decigram (dg)}$$
$$10 \text{ decigrams (dg)} = 1 \text{ gram (g)}$$
$$10 \text{ grams (g)} = 1 \text{ dekagram (dag)}$$
$$10 \text{ dekagrams (dag)} = 1 \text{ hectogram (hg)}$$
$$10 \text{ hectograms (hg)} = 1 \text{ kilogram (kg)}$$

Here again, going from the smallest to the largest measure, each differs from the previous one by a factor of ten.

The following chart will help students see the relationship between each of these measures and the gram, and show them how to make conversions between them. We will now change the popular childhood saying to: <u>K</u>ing <u>H</u>enry <u>D</u>ied <u>G</u>hastly <u>D</u>rinking <u>C</u>hocolate <u>M</u>ilk, where the first letter of each word in the saying refers to the first letter of metric mass from largest (kilogram) to smallest (milligram).

<u>K</u>ing	<u>H</u>enry	<u>D</u>ied	<u>G</u>hastly	<u>D</u>rinking	<u>C</u>hocolate	<u>M</u>ilk
kg	hg	dag	g	dg	cg	mg
kilogram	hectogram	dekagram	gram	decigram	centigram	milligram
1kg = 1000g	1hg = 100g	1dag = 10g		10dg = 1g	100cg = 1g	1000mg = 1g

From this scale, we can see that 1 kg = 1,000 g, 1 hg = 100 g, and so on. As before, the general rule is that to convert from larger units to smaller units you should multiply. Here are some examples:

Convert kilograms to grams.

$$\left.\begin{array}{lll} 3.982 \text{ kg} & = ? \text{ g} \\ 3.982 \times 1,000 & = 3982 \\ 3.982 \text{ kg} & = 3982 \text{ g} \end{array}\right\} \begin{array}{l} \text{To multiply} \\ \text{by 1,000,} \\ \text{shift decimal} \\ \text{3 to the right.} \end{array}$$

Convert grams to centigrams.

$$\left.\begin{array}{lll} 7.11 \text{ g} & = ? \text{ cg} \\ 7.11 \times 100 & = 711 \\ 7.11 \text{ g} & = 711 \text{ cg} \end{array}\right\} \begin{array}{l} \text{To multiply} \\ \text{by 100, shift} \\ \text{decimal 2 to} \\ \text{the right.} \end{array}$$

To convert from smaller units to larger units, you should divide:

Convert grams to hectograms.

$$\left.\begin{array}{lll} 62.9 \text{ g} & = ? \text{ hg} \\ 62.9 \div 100 & = .629 \\ 62.9 \text{ g} & = .629 \text{ hg} \end{array}\right\} \begin{array}{l} \text{To divide by} \\ \text{100, shift} \\ \text{decimal 2} \\ \text{to the left.} \end{array}$$

Convert milligrams to grams.

$$\left.\begin{array}{lll} 304 \text{ mg} & = ? \text{ g} \\ 304 \div 1,000 & = .304 \\ 304 \text{ mg} & = .304 \text{ g} \end{array}\right\} \begin{array}{l} \text{To divide by} \\ \text{1,000, shift} \\ \text{decimal 3} \\ \text{to the left.} \end{array}$$

Show youngsters they can convert to units not involving grams so long as they move the decimal point by the right number of places. This is illustrated in the following examples:

Convert hectograms to decigrams.

$$
\begin{array}{ll}
.857 \text{ hg} & = ? \text{ dg} \\
.857 \times 1{,}000 & = 857 \\
.857 \text{ hg} & = 857 \text{ dg}
\end{array}
\left\{
\begin{array}{l}
\text{To multiply by} \\
1{,}000, \text{ shift} \\
\text{decimal 3} \\
\text{to the right.}
\end{array}
\right.
$$

Convert milligrams to decigrams.

$$
\begin{array}{ll}
12.6 \text{ mg} & = ? \text{ dg} \\
12.6 \div 100 & = .126 \\
12.6 \text{ mg} & = .126 \text{ dg}
\end{array}
\left\{
\begin{array}{l}
\text{To divide by} \\
100, \text{ shift} \\
\text{decimal 2} \\
\text{to the left.}
\end{array}
\right.
$$

Summary

I have devoted a fair amount of space to weights and measures for several reasons. First of all, this information is very practical, and children encounter occasions to use it almost every day. Second, the arithmetic required to work with weights and measures utilizes most of the concepts presented so far. Third, and most important, I hope I have convinced both children and adults that the metric system is not foreign and complex, but extremely familiar and simple to learn. After working through all of my examples, your child should never be frightened or mystified about the metric system again!

7

Geometry

Galileo, the great Italian physicist and astronomer, had this to say about the universe: "It is written in the language of mathematics, and its characters are triangles, circles, and other geometric figures, without which it is humanly impossible to understand a single word of it; without these, one is wandering about in a dark labyrinth."

That just about sums up the importance of geometry, both to the field of mathematics and to the world at large. Everywhere we look we see things made out of geometric figures—the houses we live in, the buildings where we work and go to school, the vehicles we drive in, the bridges we drive over, and so on. If youngsters look closely, they will see that these structures are made up of combinations of circles, triangles, rectangles, squares, and so forth. The methods of mathematics are closely tied to geometry because of humans' desire to measure, understand, and manipulate the physical world they live in. This has been true from the earliest times, and will continue to be true as long as man inhabits the earth.

In this chapter, I will describe the basic building blocks of geometry, such as lines, rays, angles, and planes, and show how they can be combined to produce triangles, rectangles, squares, circles, and other geometrical figures. I will then explore various properties of these figures (such as congruence and symmetry) and various ways to manipulate them (such as translations, rotations, and reflections). Following this, I will explore how to measure the distance around these geometrical figures (perimeter) and how to calculate their respective area or volume. I will also show an application of the Pythagorean Theorem.

Basic Building Blocks

Here are the basic building blocks of geometric figures.

A *point* is a specific location in space.

Point A   . A

A *line* is a straight path of points that extends infinitely in two directions. (The arrows mean that it goes on forever.)

Line AB, or $\overleftrightarrow{AB}$

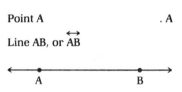

A *line segment* is the part of the line that begins at one endpoint and ends at another one. (No arrows.)

Line segment AB, or $\overline{AB}$

A *ray* is the part of the line that starts at an endpoint and extends infinitely in one direction. (One arrow.)

Ray AB, or $\overrightarrow{AB}$

An *angle* is a figure formed by two rays that have a common endpoint. This endpoint is called the vertex, and each ray called a side of the angle. An angle can be named by its vertex, or by three points with the vertex in the middle. (Use ∠ for angle.)

Angle (∠) A, ∠BAC, ∠CAB

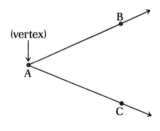

A *plane* is a flat surface that extends infinitely in all directions.

Plane x

Angles

Angles can have many different sizes, depending upon the amount of space between their two sides. We measure this space in degrees (°) using a device called a protractor, which children are usually introduced to early in school. A protractor is shaped like a semi-circle and has its degrees marked along the outer edge from lowest (at the right) to highest (at the left). In the following example, I put the center of the protractor on the vertex of the angle, line up one side of the angle with zero degrees, and read the measure of the angle by where the other side crosses the same scale:

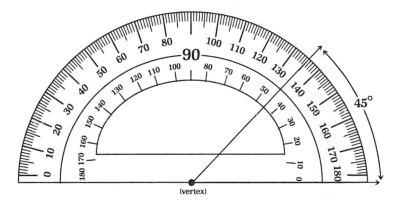

(vertex)

There are four basic types of angles, which are categorized by the number of degrees they have:

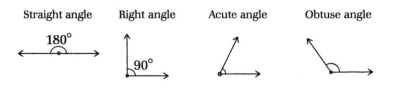

Straight angle	Right angle	Acute angle	Obtuse angle
180°	90°		
Has exactly 180°	Has exactly 90°	Has less than 90°	Has more than 90° and less than 180°

Lines

We have discussed individual lines already, but students should also understand relationships between two lines:

Parallel lines are lines in a plane that never cross (intersect). (In the example to the right, $\overline{AB}$ is parallel ($\|$) to $\overline{CD}$.

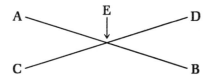

Intersecting lines are lines in a plane that cross each other. (In the example to the right, $\overline{AB}$ intersects $\overline{CD}$ at E.)

Perpendicular lines are lines in a plane that intersect each other and form right angles. (In the example to the right, $\overline{AB}$ is perpendicular ($\perp$) to $\overline{CD}$.)

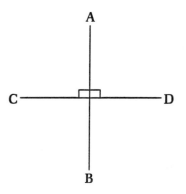

Now that we have examined various relationships between angles and lines, we are ready to explore the basic geometric figures and their properties. We will be discussing various polygons and the circle. A polygon is a figure whose sides are made up of line segments. Polygons are "closed figures" because there are no openings around their boundaries. Polygons can be classified based on the number of sides they have. The first figure we will consider is the triangle.

Triangles

A triangle is a three-sided polygon. There are various types of triangles, which can be classified by both the length of their sides and the measures of their angles.

Triangles classified by the length of their sides.

Equilateral triangle.   Isosceles triangle.

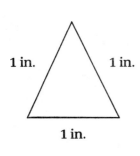

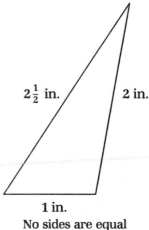

All sides are equal.   At least two sides are equal.

Scalene triangle.

No sides are equal

Triangles classified by the measures of their angles.

Right triangle.   Acute triangle.

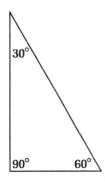

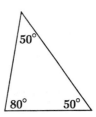

Has one right angle.   Has three acute angles.

Obtuse triangle.

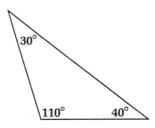

Has one obtuse angle.

One feature common to all triangles is that their three angles add up to 180°. (You can convince yourself of this fact by cutting out the three angles of any triangle and putting them together, which produces a straight angle of 180°.) This fact enables one to solve for the measure of a third angle in a triangle when the other two angles are given. For example, if a triangle has angle A equal to 50° and angle B equal to 60°, what is the measure of angle C?

Find ∠C.

∠C + 50° + 60° = 180°

∠C + 110°   = 180°

∠C   = 180° − 110°

∠C   = 70°

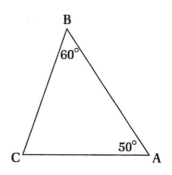

Quadrilaterals

Quadrilaterals are four-sided polygons. Some quadrilaterals have special names that correspond to their shapes:

A parallelogram has two pairs of parallel sides and two pairs of equal sides.

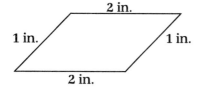

A rectangle is a parallelogram that has four right angles (four 90° angles).

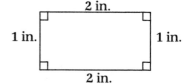

A rhombus is a parallelogram that has four equal sides.

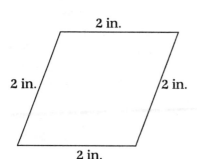

A square is a rectangle that has four equal sides.

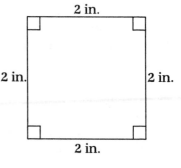

A trapezoid is a polygon that has exactly one pair of parallel sides.

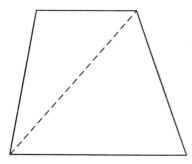

A common feature of all quadrilaterals is that the sum of their four angles equals 360°. To show this to children, draw a diagonal line that connects two vertices of the quadrilateral. This produces two triangles (see diagram at the left). They know that the sum of angles in two triangles equals 360°, because the angles in each triangle add up to 180°.

Other Polygons

Students should know that there are other polygons that have five sides, six sides, seven sides, and so on. When the sides are exactly the same length, we refer to these figures as regular polygons. Here are some examples of the more popular ones:

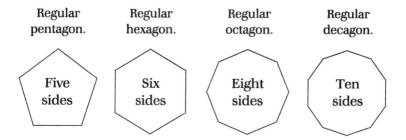

| Regular pentagon. | Regular hexagon. | Regular octagon. | Regular decagon. |
| Five sides | Six sides | Eight sides | Ten sides |

Circles

A circle is a geometric figure made up of all the points in a plane that are the same distance from the center. There are several different parts of a circle that have specific names.

These are illustrated below:

A *chord* is a line segment that has both endpoints on the circle. AB is a chord.

The *diameter* is a chord that passes through the center of the circle. CD is a diameter.

The *radius* is a line segment that joins the center of the circle with any point on the circle. EF is a radius. (Note that the radius is half the length of the diameter.)

The *tangent* is a line that intersects the circle at exactly one point. The point of tangency occurs at point G.

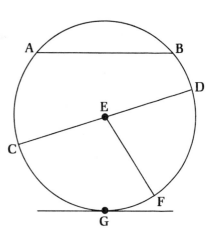

Properties of Geometric Figures

Three important properties that occur when comparing two or more geometric figures are congruence, similarity, and symmetry:

Figures are said to be *congruent* when they have exactly the same shape and size. All of their corresponding angles and sides are congruent. The two figures below are congruent (≅):

The corresponding angles are congruent:
∠A ≅ ∠D, ∠B ≅ ∠E, ∠C ≅ ∠F

The corresponding sides are congruent:
$\overline{AB} \cong \overline{DE}$, $\overline{BC} \cong \overline{EF}$, $\overline{CA} \cong \overline{FD}$

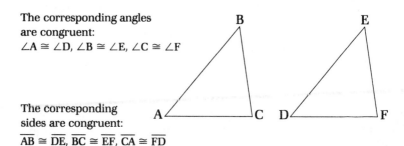

Figures are said to be *similar* when they have exactly the same shape, but not necessarily the same size. All of the corresponding angles are congruent, and the ratios of lengths of corresponding sides are congruent. The two figures below are similar:

The corresponding angles are congruent:
∠G ≅ ∠J, ∠H ≅ ∠K, ∠I ≅ ∠L

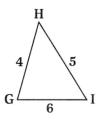

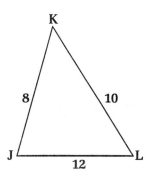

The ratios of the lengths of corresponding sides are equal:

$$\frac{\text{Length of } \overline{GH}}{\text{Length of } \overline{JK}} \quad \frac{4}{8} = \frac{5}{10} \quad \frac{\text{Length of } \overline{HI}}{\text{Length of } \overline{KL}}$$

Figures are said to be *symmetrical* if one half of a figure would exactly fit over the other half when folded over a line of symmetry. In the figures below, the dotted line represents the line(s) of symmetry:

Acute triangle.	Isosceles triangle.	Rectangle.	Equilateral triangle.

No lines of symmetry	One line of symmetry	Two lines of symmetry	Three lines of symmetry

Operations With Geometric Figures

There are three different operations with geometric figures.

These are translation, reflection, and rotation:

Figures are said to be *translated* when they can be moved in a path along a straight line:

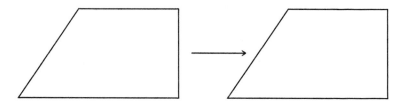

Figures are said to be *reflected* when they are flipped across a line of symmetry:

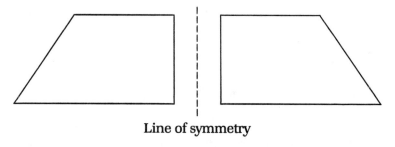

Line of symmetry

Figures are said to be *rotated* when they are turned on a curved path around a point:

Point of rotation

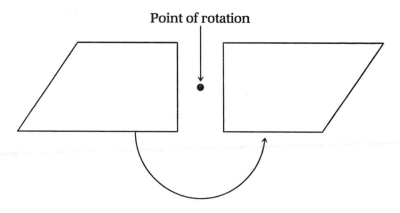

Now that your child is knowledgeable about the basic geometric figures and their various properties, we will examine the concepts of perimeter (and circumference), area, and volume. The perimeter is just the distance around the boundary of the various polygons we have been discussing, while the circumference is the distance around a circle. The area represents the amount of space these geometrical figures occupy. We will examine a special type of area called surface area, which applies to figures in three-dimensional space. The surface area is the amount of space occupied by the outside surface of these figures. Volume also applies to geometric figures in three-dimensional space and can be thought of as the amount of some substance that these figures will hold. To assist children in the discussion, I will introduce several new three-dimensional geometric figures and provide handy formulae that make it easy to calculate these new concepts.

Perimeter

The most direct way of finding the perimeter (or the distance around) for any polygon is to add up the lengths of each of its sides. For example, to find the perimeter (P) of the following trapezoid, we simply sum the lengths of all four sides:

P = sum of the lengths of all four
     sides
P = 6 + 6 + 6 + 12
P = 30 feet

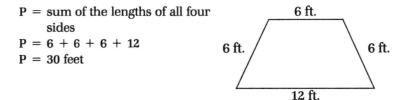

The distance around the trapezoid is 30 feet.

When calculating the perimeter of a rectangle, we can take advantage of the fact that it has two pairs of congruent sides.

This enables us to use the following formula for calculating the perimeter of a rectangle:

P = (2 × length) +
     (2 × width) = 2l + 2w
P = (2 × 21) + (2 × 17)
P = 42 + 34
P = 76 meters

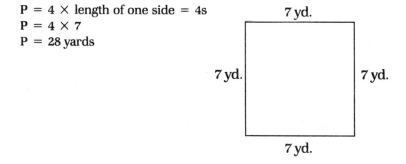

The distance around the rectangle is 76 meters.

To calculate the perimeter of a square, we can take advantage of the fact that a square has four sides of equal length. To obtain the perimeter of a square with each side equal to 7 yards, all we need to do is multiply the length of one side (s) by four:

P = 4 × length of one side = 4s
P = 4 × 7
P = 28 yards

The distance around the square is 28 yards.

Circumference

To show children how to calculate the circumference of, or distance around, a circle, you will need to employ the concept of pi, which is represented by the Greek letter π. Although π may seem mysterious, it is nothing more than the ratio of the circumference of a circle to its diameter. This ratio, which is the same for all circles, is equal to approximately $\frac{22}{7}$ or 3.14.

Since the ratio of the circumference (C) of a circle to its diameter (d) equals π, we can multiply each side of the equation by d to solve for the circumference:

$\frac{C}{d} = \pi$, so $d \times \frac{C}{d} = \pi \times d$, or $C = \pi \times d$, which is often written as $C = \pi d$.

Since the diameter equals two times the radius (r), we can also say that:

$$C = \pi \times 2 \times r, \text{ or } C = 2 \times \pi \times r, \text{ or simply } C = 2\pi r.$$

Since 3.14 and $\frac{22}{7}$ are only approximate values for π, we can indicate this when making calculations by the symbol ($\approx$), which means "is approximately equal to."

As an example, show your child how to use these formulae to find the circumference of a circle with a diameter equal to 14 inches (or, alternatively, a radius equal to 7 inches)

$$C = \pi \times d \qquad\qquad C = 2 \times \pi \times r$$

$$C \approx 3.14 \times 14 \quad \text{or} \quad C \approx 2 \times \frac{22}{\overset{}{\underset{1}{7}}} \times \overset{1}{7}$$

$$C \approx 43.96 \text{ inches} \qquad C \approx 44 \text{ inches}$$

Thus, the circumference of the circle is approximately equal to 44 inches. We can see that the estimate is approximate because the two approaches yield slightly different results.

Area

The best way to explain the concept of area to children is to ask the question, "How many squares with sides equal to one unit will fit into a given polygon?" For example, if we want to know the area of a rectangle that is 6 feet by 3 feet, we can see that the rectangle holds exactly 18 squares that have sides equal to 1 foot:

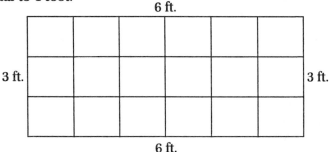

The appropriate way to express the area of this rectangle is 18 square feet.

Area of Rectangles and Squares

Obviously we do not want to draw squares of unit length every time we need to calculate the area of a polygon. For rectangles and squares, there are straightforward formulae we can use.

Rectangles have two pairs of equal sides, so we can multiply their length (l) by their width (w) to find the area (A):

A = length × width, or
     simply A = lw
A =   4   ×   2
A =   8 square feet

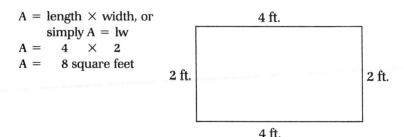

The area of the rectangle is 8 square feet.

We can write 8 square feet as 8 ft^2, where the number 2 is called an exponent. The exponent 2 indicates that a value (in this problem, feet) is being multiplied by itself (4 ft $\times$ 2 ft = 8 ft^2). In a similar manner, 10 $\times$ 10 = 10^2. If a value is multiplied by itself 3 times we would use the exponent 3; if multiplied by itself 4 times the exponent would be 4, and so on. Explain to your child that exponents are just a shorthand way of writing an expression. I will have a lot more to say about exponents in the next chapter, Algebra I.

Squares have four equal sides (s), so we can multiply one side by another to find the area (A) of a square. (Notice the use of the exponent 2, because we are multiplying one side (s) by another side (s) of the same length):

$A = \text{side} \times \text{side, or } A = s \times s = s^2$
$A = \quad 3 \quad \times \quad 3$
$A = \quad 9 \text{ ft}^2$

3 ft.

3 ft.

The area of the square is 9 square feet, or 9 ft^2.

Area of Parallelograms and Triangles

Now that your child knows how to calculate the area of a rectangle, it is relatively straightforward for her to figure out how to calculate the area of a parallelogram. For any parallelogram, we can reconfigure it to look like a rectangle. All we need to do is cut one triangular end off of the parallelogram, and by attaching it to the other end we have made a rectangle:

A parallelogram . . .   reconfigured to look like a rectangle.

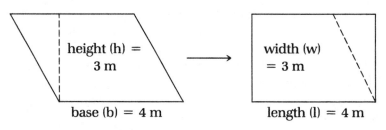

This should convince your youngster that the parallelogram and the rectangle have the same area. All we need now is a formula that tells us how to calculate the area of the parallelogram.

Your child already knows that the formula for calculating the area of a rectangle is:

$$A = length \times width, or A = lw$$

She should now be able to see that the formula for calculating the area of the parallelogram is:

$$A = base \times height, or A = bh$$

Thus, we can calculate the area of the parallelogram above by plugging values into the following formula:

$$A = base \times height$$
$$A = 4m \times 3m$$
$$A = 12 \ m^2$$

The area of the parallelogram (and rectangle) is $12 \ m^2$.

Now that your child understands how to calculate the area of a parallelogram, it is also straightforward for her to figure out how to calculate the area of a triangle. By drawing a diagonal line through any parallelogram, we can divide it into two congruent triangles. Using the same parallelogram shown above:

The diagonal line divides the parallelogram into two congruent triangles.

height (h) = 3 m

base (b) = 4 m

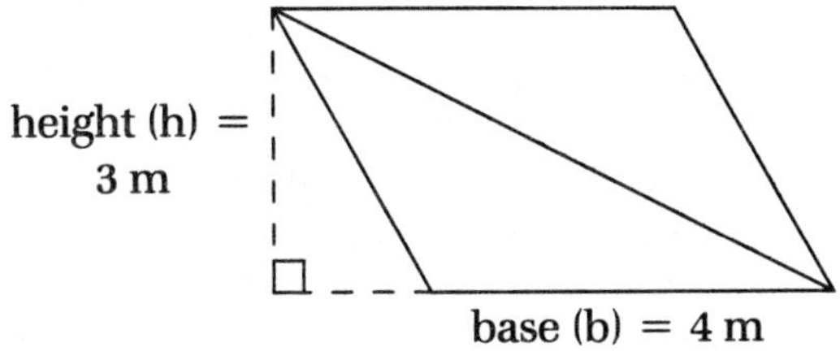

Now, since the area of the parallelogram is:

$A = $ base $\times$ height

it should be clear that the area of each triangle is:

$A = \dfrac{1}{2} \times$ base $\times$ height

To figure out the area of one of the triangles, all we have to do is plug the values into the formula:

$A = \dfrac{1}{2} \times$ base $\times$ height

$A = \dfrac{1}{2} \times \ 4 \ \times \ 3$

$A = \dfrac{1}{\cancel{2}} \times \overset{6}{\cancel{12}}$

$A = 6 \ m^2$

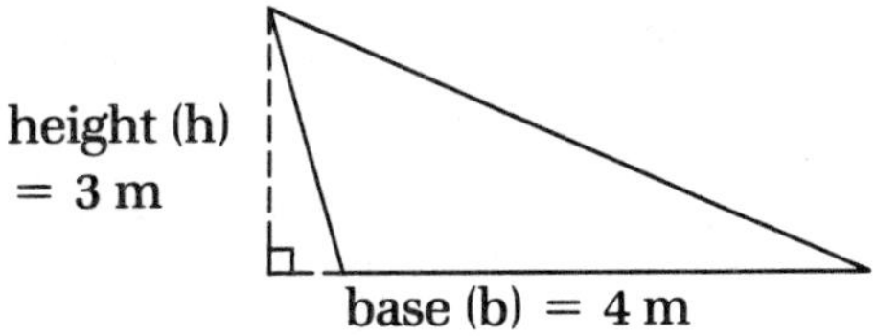

height (h) = 3 m

base (b) = 4 m

The area of one of the triangles equals 6 m².

Area of a Circle

Your child may be surprised to learn that knowing how to calculate the area of a parallelogram helps in understanding how to calculate the area of a circle. To illustrate why, consider the following pie, which is divided into six equal slices.

We can rearrange the slices of pie to look something like a parallelogram:

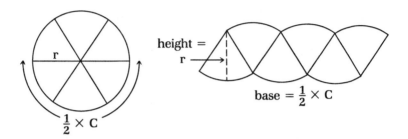

Thus, the area of the circle closely approximates the area of the parallelogram.

Point out to your child that the base of the figure that looks like a parallelogram is one-half of the circumference (C) of the pie (circle), because it is made up of three slices of pie. The height of the figure is equal to the length of one piece of pie (which is the radius of the circle). Thus, the area of the parallelogram is:

$$A = \text{base} \times \text{height}$$

$$A = \frac{1}{2} \times C \times r$$

But since $C = 2\pi r$, $A = \frac{1}{2} \times 2\pi r \times r$

or, $A = \pi r^2$

Since the area of the circle is approximately equal to the area of the parallelogram, the area of a circle is approximately equal to πr^2.

Let's now apply this knowledge to calculate the area of a circle. Here is how we would find the area of a circle with a radius equal to 7 inches:

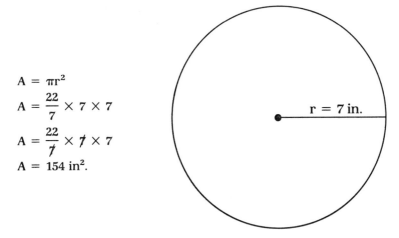

$A = \pi r^2$

$A = \dfrac{22}{7} \times 7 \times 7$

$A = \dfrac{22}{\cancel{7}} \times \cancel{7} \times 7$

$A = 154 \text{ in}^2.$

The area of the circle equals 154 in².

Pythagorean Theorem

One of the most important theorems in mathematics is the Pythagorean Theorem. (A theorem is nothing more than a generalization that can be demonstrated to be true.) Pythagoras was a mathematician who lived in ancient Greece around the time of 500 B.C. His theorem allows you to find the length of any side of a right triangle, given the lengths of the other two sides. Before stating his theorem, it is useful for students to consider the following right triangle:

Side a is called a leg of the triangle.
Side b is also called a leg of the triangle.
Side c is called the hypotenuse of the
    triangle.

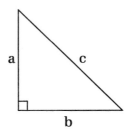

The Pythagorean Theorem states that, for any given right triangle, the square of the length of the hypotenuse equals the sum of the squares of the lengths of the other two legs. Symbolically, we can represent this relationship as:

$$c^2 = a^2 + b^2$$

Here is an example for your child to consider. Calculate the length of the hypotenuse for the right triangle shown below:

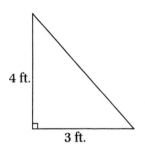

$c^2 = a^2 + b^2$
$c^2 = (4)^2 + (3)^2$
$c^2 = 16 + 9$
$c^2 = 25$
$c = 5$ ft (because $5 \times 5 = 25$)

4 ft.

3 ft.

Point out to your youngster that he can solve for the length of side a if he is given the lengths of sides b and c, by making the following adjustments to the formula:

$c^2 = a^2 + b^2$	(original formula)
$c^2 - b^2 = a^2 + b^2 - b^2$	(subtract b^2 from both sides)
$c^2 - b^2 = a^2$	(this is what is left)
$a^2 = c^2 - b^2$	(which can also be stated like this)

By subtracting a^2 from both sides of the original equation, in the same manner, he can derive that:

$$b^2 = c^2 - a^2$$

Thus, using the appropriate formula, he can find the length of any side of a right triangle if he knows the lengths of the other two sides. Your child will have frequent occasion to use the Pythagorean Theorem as he advances further in the subject of mathematics; he can use this theorem to find the distance between two points and in many other applications as well.

Solid (Three-Dimensional) Figures

So far, you have shown your child a variety of geometric figures in a two-dimensional plane, like the piece of paper you are looking at now. As we move into three-dimensional (or solid) figures, we have to consider not only length and width, but also height. We will consider some of the more common solid geometrical figures and then discuss how to calculate surface area and volume for them.

Solid figures having faces that are polygons, such as those we have already considered, are called polyhedrons. One of the groups in this category is the prism. Prisms can be identified by the shapes of their bases. Here are three common prisms you can show your child:

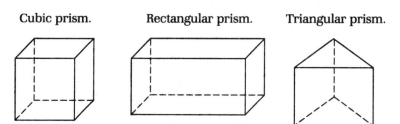

Cubic prism.   Rectangular prism.   Triangular prism.

Notice that the bases (tops and bottoms) of each prism are congruent.

Pyramids may look like prisms at first glance, but if you inspect them carefully you will see that they do not have tops and bottoms that are congruent. In fact, their tops come to a sharp point. The two types of pyramids are named by the shapes of their bottom bases:

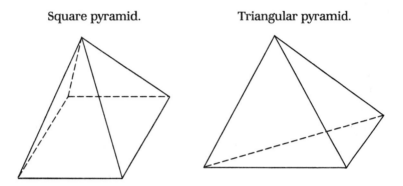

Square pyramid.   Triangular pyramid.

Students should know about another class of solid figures that are not polyhedrons because their faces are not polygons. What they have in common is that some part of their structure involves a circle (or circles):

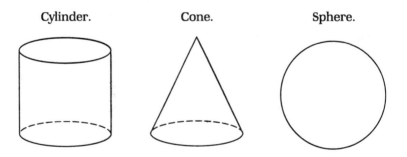

Cylinder.   Cone.   Sphere.

Surface Area

The surface area of a solid figure is just the total area of all of the exterior sides (or faces) of the figure. To compute the surface area, we find the area of each face and then add up these amounts. As an example, suppose we want to find the surface area of a box that is shaped like a cube. If we can visualize the cube when it is unfolded and laid out flat on the ground, we can see how many faces there are and the dimensions of each face:

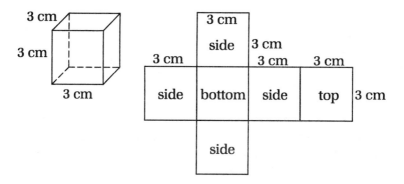

Since each face of the cube is a square, the area (A) of each face is obtained by multiplying a side (s) by a side (s), and the total surface area (SA) is obtained by adding up the area of the six faces:

Area of each face.

$A = s \times s = s^2$
$A = 3 \times 3$
$A = 9 \text{ cm}^2.$

Total surface area.

$SA = 6 \times A$
$SA = 6 \times 9 \text{ cm}^2.$
$SA = 54 \text{ cm}^2.$

The total surface area of the cube is 54 cm².

In a similar manner, we can calculate the surface area of the cylinder. Notice that if we take the cylinder apart, and lay it out along the ground, we have two circles and a rectangle:

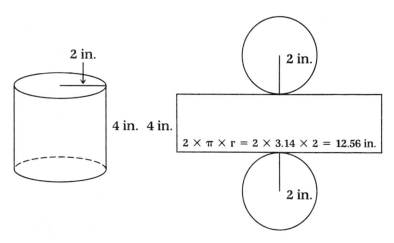

Thus, to calculate the surface area of the cylinder, we find the area of both circles, and add this to the area of the rectangle. (Notice that the length of the rectangle equals the circumference of the circle ($2 \times \pi \times r$). Ask your youngster to imagine taking the label off a soup can and then wrapping it back around the can. The label fits right around the top and bottom of the can, which is the circumference of the circle:

Area of a circle.	Area of two circles.	Area of a rectangle.	Surface area.
$A = \pi \times r^2$	$A \approx 2 \times 12.56$ in².	$A = l \times w$	
$A \approx 3.14 \times 2 \times 2$	$A \approx 25.12$ in².	$A = (2 \times \pi \times r) \times w$	25.12 in².
$A \approx 12.56$ in².		$A = 2 \times 3.14 \times 2 \times 4$	+50.24 in².
		$A = 50.24$ in².	75.36 in².

The total surface area of the cylinder is 75.36 in².

Volume

To help your child understand the concept of volume, you can return to the earlier example showing how to find the area of a rectangle. Suppose that we now have a rectangular prism with the same length (6 ft) and width (3 ft) as the earlier rectangle, but now it has a height of 2 ft. The relevant question to ask your child is, "How many cubes that measure 1 ft by 1 ft by 1 ft will fit into the rectangular prism?" We can represent this as follows:

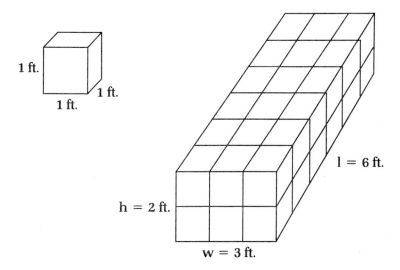

By counting them up, it should be obvious that 36 cubes fit into the rectangular prism.

Here again, emphasize that we do not want to have to count up all of the cubes that will fit into a rectangular prism to calculate its volume (V). Instead, we can calculate the volume very quickly by multiplying its length by its width by its height. For the rectangular prism above:

$$V = \text{length} \times \text{width} \times \text{height, or } V = lwh$$
$$V = 6 \times 3 \times 2$$
$$V = 36 \text{ cubic feet} = 36 \text{ ft}^3$$

The volume of the rectangular prism above is 36 ft^3.

It should now be obvious to your child that a cubic prism, or cube, is just a special type of rectangular prism in which all of the sides are of the same length. Accordingly, we can find the volume of a cube by multiplying the length of each side that corresponds to its length, width, and height (which is the same as multiplying side by side by side):

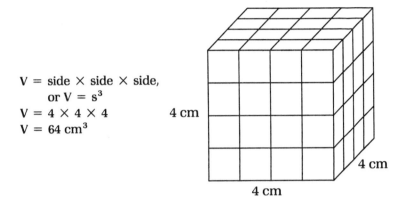

$$V = \text{side} \times \text{side} \times \text{side},$$
$$\text{or } V = s^3$$
$$V = 4 \times 4 \times 4 \qquad 4\text{ cm}$$
$$V = 64 \text{ cm}^3$$

4 cm

4 cm

4 cm

The volume of the cube is 64 cm^3.

Summary

In this chapter we have reviewed a number of geometric figures in both two- and three-dimensional space. We have described their properties, shown how to perform operations with them, and discussed how to calculate various measures such as perimeter, area, surface area, and volume. The emphasis has been on concepts rather than practical applications, so your child will know not only what the appropriate formulae are, but will also understand how they are derived. Most of the practical applications involving geometric figures are very straightforward, as you and your youngster will have an opportunity to see in subsequent chapters.

8

Algebra I

Algebra may seem very confusing to children and adults but, actually, it is very straightforward once we realize that it is nothing more than a logical extension of basic arithmetic. With arithmetic we learn how to perform fundamental operations with numbers, like addition, subtraction, multiplication, and division. Algebra involves the same fundamental operations with numbers, but also uses letters to represent some of the numbers. If your child has mastered the basic arithmetic operations presented earlier, then he or she will have a good foundation for learning algebra.

Basic Concepts

In earlier chapters, we considered a selected set of numbers. First, we talked about the *natural numbers,* or counting numbers, such as 1,2,3,4,5,6,7,8,9,10, and so on. We can represent the *set* of natural numbers, by using brackets, as {1,2,3,4,5 . . .}, where . . . means "and so on." If we add 0 to the set of natural numbers we have the set of *whole numbers,* which we can represent as {0,1,2,3,4,5 . . .}. In addition to whole numbers, we also considered decimals, fractions, and mixed numbers.

Now it is time to introduce your youngster to the concept of *negative numbers*—in other words, numbers less than zero. Negative numbers can be integers, fractions, or decimals. The best way to represent all of the different types of numbers we have talked about so far is through the use of a *number line*:

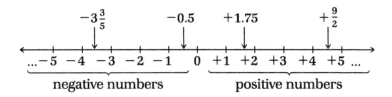

There are a few things to point out about this number line. I have designated all numbers less than 0 on the number line as negative numbers, and all numbers greater than 0 as positive numbers. Notice that the negative numbers are always preceeded by a minus sign (e.g., -5 is read as minus 5). Although I have designated the positive numbers with a plus sign $(+)$, for illustration, it is not always necessary to write it (e.g., $+5$ can be written as just 5). I have also included a few decimal and fractional numbers on the number line for illustration, although I could have chosen other numbers to show as well. In fact, there are an infinite quantity (as large as you can imagine) of numbers along this number line, because I could represent both fractions as decimals with finer levels of precision. The positive and negative numbers together are referred to as *signed numbers*.

Now you should show your child how to analyze the numbers along the number line more carefully. As we move to the right along the number line, the numbers get larger. And as we move to the left along the number line, the numbers get smaller. Thus, any number to the right of another number is larger than that number, and any number to the left of another number is smaller than that number. To illustrate this idea, remember the terminology we introduced earlier, where $(<)$ means less than, $(=)$ means equal to, and $(>)$ means greater than.

Here are some examples you can show your youngster that make comparisons of numbers along the number line. (Look back at the number line as you read these comparisons):

$$-5 < -3 \qquad -2 > -6$$
$$-3 < 0 \qquad 0 > -1$$
$$-1 < 8 \qquad 3 > -4$$
$$3 < 6 \qquad 5 > 2$$

Let's make some more observations about fractions, so we will have a complete understanding of them. Any number that can be written as a fraction is called a *rational number*. In an earlier chapter we also saw that any fraction can be written as a decimal by dividing the numerator by the denominator. When we make this division, there are two possibilities: the decimal (quotient) is either terminating or repeating. Here are some examples of each:

Terminating Decimal   Repeating Decimal

$$\frac{1}{4} = 4\overline{)1.00} \quad \frac{.25}{ } = .25 \qquad \frac{4}{11} = 11\overline{)4.0000} \quad \frac{.3636}{ } = .363636...$$

Terminating	Repeating
$\underline{8}$	$\underline{3\,3}$
20	70
$\underline{20}$	$\underline{66}$
0	40
	$\underline{33}$
	70
	$\underline{66}$

If a decimal is neither terminating nor repeating, then it is said to be an *irrational number*. In fact, irrational numbers cannot even be written as fractions. A good example of an irrational number is $\pi = 3.14159...$ which we discussed earlier when talking about relationships of circles. The set of rational and irrational numbers together make up *real numbers*. Real numbers consist of all the different types of numbers we have been discussing so far, such as natural numbers, whole numbers, decimals, fractions, and mixed numbers. They include negative numbers, positive numbers, and zero. In summary, real numbers are numbers that can be represented on the number line.

Arithmetic Operations Involving Signed Numbers

Addition. Students will need to know how to add signed numbers. This can be represented by using the number line. In general, positive numbers can be shown as a rightward movement along the number line, and negative numbers can be shown as a leftward movement along the number line. For example, suppose we want to add 1 and 3 together. We start at 0 and move 1 to the right, and from this position we move another 3 to the right. The answer is seen to be 4:

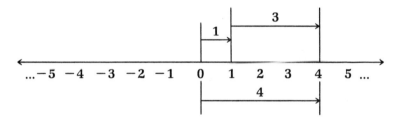

Now suppose we want to add -5 to 3. This can also be represented on the number line. We start at 0 and move 3 to the right, and from there we move 5 to the left. The answer is -2:

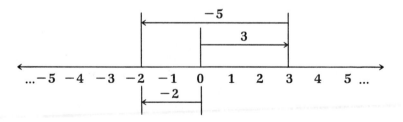

Now, as a final example, suppose we want to add -2 and -3 together. We start at 0 and move 2 to the left, and from there we move another 3 to the left. The answer is −5:

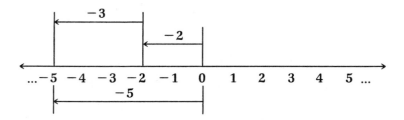

One more concept will be useful for your child to know, and that is the concept of the *absolute value* of a number. The absolute value of a number is the distance on the number line between 0 and the number, without regard for direction. The absolute value of a number, which is indicated by two vertical lines around the number (| |), can never be negative. Let's look at the absolute value of 4 (|4|) and −4 (|−4|) on the number line:

Note that |4| = |−4| = 4. Although not illustrated here, it should also be noted that |0| = 0.

When looking at signed numbers, emphasize that the absolute value of the number can be distinguished from its sign:

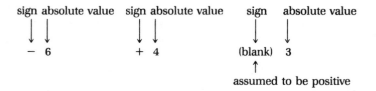

Reference to a number line is very useful for helping children to understand how to add signed numbers but, obviously, we do not want to go through this lengthy process every time we need to add signed numbers. For this reason, here are some simple rules that will help your youngster perform these additions:

Rule 1: To add two numbers with the *same sign,* add their absolute values and assign the same sign to their sum.

Add the absolute values together

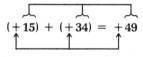

and assign the sum the same sign.

Add the absolute values together

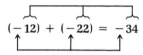

and assign the sum the same sign.

Rule 2: To add two numbers with *different signs,* subtract the smaller absolute value from the larger one, and assign the sum the same sign as the number with the larger absolute value.

Subtract the smaller absolute value from the larger one,

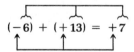

and assign the sum the same sign as the number with the larger absolute value.

Subtract the smaller absolute value from the larger one,

$$(-15) + (+4) = -11$$

and assign the sum the same sign as the number with the larger absolute value.

Tell your child that the same rules also apply to arithmetic operations involving the addition of signed decimals and signed fractions. To make sure that she has mastered these rules, let's consider some examples of each:

Add the following signed decimals:

$(+7.3472) + (+4.1008) = +11.4480$ $(-23.56) + (-14.79) = -38.35$

$(-2.139) + (+8.182) = +6.043$ $(-45.1) + (+21.8) = -23.3$

Fractions. When students are working with fractions, it is important for them to recognize that every fraction has three signs. There is the sign of the fraction, the sign of the numerator, and the sign of the denominator. For example, consider the following fraction:

sign of the numerator

sign of the fraction $\longrightarrow +\dfrac{-3}{+5}$

sign of the denominator

If two of the three signs of a fraction are changed, the value of the fraction remains the same. For example, all of the following fractions are equivalent:

$$+\left(\frac{-3}{5}\right) = +\left(\frac{3}{-5}\right) = -\left(\frac{-3}{-5}\right) = -\left(\frac{3}{5}\right)$$

This rule produces results that are consistent with the rules of multiplication and division of signed numbers presented earlier. Your youngster can evaluate any of the fractions shown above, and he will see that they are all equivalent.

Add the following signed fractions:

$\left(+6\frac{1}{4}\right) + \left(+8\frac{2}{4}\right) = +14\frac{3}{4}$ $\left(\frac{-3}{2}\right) + \left(\frac{-5}{2}\right) = \frac{-8}{2} = -4$

$\left(\frac{-3}{7}\right) + \left(\frac{+5}{7}\right) = \frac{+2}{7}$ $\left(-7\frac{2}{3}\right) + \left(+2\frac{1}{3}\right) = -5\frac{1}{3}$

Subtraction. To discuss the subtraction of signed numbers, you can build upon what you already know about the addition of signed numbers. Let's first take a look at what we mean by subtraction. To understand subtraction, you have to know how to find the opposite of a number. To find the opposite of a number, you simply change its sign. (For example, the opposite of 5 is -5.) When we subtract one number from another, this is the same as adding the opposite of the number to it. Let's look at an example:

Subtracting 3 from 5 is the same as adding
the opposite of 3 (-3) to 5.

$$5 - 3 = 5 + (-3) = 2$$

This suggests a rule that we can use to subtract signed numbers, which allows us to use the methods we already know for adding signed numbers:

Rule: To subtract one signed number from another one, change the subtraction symbol to addition and change the sign of the number being subtracted. Then proceed as when adding signed numbers.

Here are a couple of examples you can use to illustrate the concept:

Original problem.		Change the subtraction symbol to addition and change the sign of the number being subtracted.		Then proceed as in the addition of signed numbers.
$(+9) - (+4)$	$=$	$(+9) + (-4)$	$=$	$+5$
$(+9) - (-4)$	$=$	$(+9) + (+4)$	$=$	$+13$
$(-9) - (+4)$	$=$	$(-9) + (-4)$	$=$	-13
$(-9) - (-4)$	$=$	$(-9) + (+4)$	$=$	-5

Note that in the preceding examples, I have added parentheses and plus signs to make the calculations easier to understand. For example, in the first example, $(+9) - (+4)$ is the same as $9 - 4$. In the third example, $(-9) - (+4)$ is the same as $-9 - 4$. Students need to become familiar with both methods of expression.

The same rules also apply when performing subtraction of signed decimals and signed fractions. Here are some examples you can use to illustrate the approach:

Subtract the following signed decimals:

$$(+8.732) - (+3.614) = (+8.732) + (-3.614) = +5.118$$

$$(+6.12) - (-2.29) = (+6.12) + (+2.29) = +8.41$$

Subtract the following signed fractions:

$$\left(-3\frac{3}{5}\right) - \left(+2\frac{1}{5}\right) = \left(-3\frac{3}{5}\right) + \left(-2\frac{1}{5}\right) = -5\frac{4}{5}$$

$$\left(\frac{-6}{7}\right) - \left(\frac{-3}{7}\right) = \left(\frac{-6}{7}\right) + \left(\frac{+3}{7}\right) = \frac{-3}{7}$$

Multiplication. Before you discuss the multiplication of signed numbers with your child, you should explain that the operation of multiplication can be expressed in several ways. Up until now, we have expressed the multiplication of two numbers with an x between them, such as $3 \times 5 = 15$. The multiplication of 3 and 5 can be expressed in the following ways:

$$3 \times 5 = 15 \qquad 3 \cdot 5 = 15 \qquad 3(5) = 15 \qquad (3)(5) = 15$$

You may see any of these variations of multiplication in the examples that follow.

To help children understand the rules for multiplying signed numbers, you can make some observations. If we multiply two positive numbers together, such as 3×4, this is just a shorthand method of doing repeated addition of the same number: $3 \times 4 = 4 + 4 + 4 = 12$. This suggests that multiplying two positive numbers together yields a product with a positive sign. If we multiply a positive number by a negative number, such as $3 \times (-4)$, this is the same as saying: $3 \times (-4) = (-4) + (-4) + (-4) = -12$. This suggests that multiplying two numbers with different signs yields a product with a negative sign. Finally, if we multiply two negative numbers together, such as $(-3) \times (-4)$, we can rearrange this multiplication to figure out the sign of the product:

$$
\begin{aligned}
(-3)(-4) &= (-1)(3)(-4) && \text{Because } -3 = (-1)(3) \\
&= (-1)(-12) && \text{Because } (3)(-4) = -12 \\
&= \text{opposite of } -12 && \text{Because multiplying a number} \\
& && \text{by } -1 \text{ yields the opposite of} \\
& && \text{the number.} \\
&= 12 && \text{Because the opposite of } -12 \\
& && \text{is 12}
\end{aligned}
$$

This suggests that multiplying two negative numbers together yields a product with a positive sign.

The preceding examples suggest the following rule for multiplying two signed numbers together:

Rule: To multiply two signed numbers together, first multiply their absolute values together. The product will be positive if the two numbers have the same sign. The product will be negative if the two numbers have different signs.

Here are some examples you can use to illustrate multiplication involving signed numbers:

$(5)(6) = 30 \quad (-8)(7) = -56 \quad (2)(-24) = -48 \quad (-9)(-9) = 81$

The same rule also applies to the multiplication of decimals,

$$(2.35)(6.82) \ = \ 16.027 \qquad (-4.39)(3.79) \ = \ -16.6381$$

. . . and fractions:

$$\left(-\frac{3}{5}\right)\left(\frac{10}{9}\right) \ = \ -\frac{30}{45} \ = \ -\frac{2}{3} \qquad \left(-\frac{16}{3}\right)\left(-\frac{9}{4}\right) \ = \ \frac{144}{12} \ = \ 12$$

Division. Division should be easy for children because the rules for dividing signed numbers are the same as the rules they used for multiplying signed numbers. To realize this, we will consider some examples:

$(5)(2) \ = \ 10$ implies that $5 = \dfrac{10}{2}$ $\qquad$ $(-5)(2) \ = \ -10$ implies that $-5 = \dfrac{-10}{2}$

$(5)(-2) \ = \ -10$ implies that $5 = \dfrac{-10}{-2}$ $\quad$ $(-5)(-2) \ = \ 10$ implies that $-5 = \dfrac{10}{-2}$

These examples lead to the following rule for dividing signed numbers:

Rule: When dividing one signed number by another, first divide their absolute values. The quotient is positive if the signed numbers have the same sign, and the quotient is negative if the signed numbers have different signs.

Here are some examples you can use to illustrate the rule:

$$(+72) \ \div \ (+9) \ = \ +8 \qquad (-49) \ \div \ (+7) \ = \ -7$$

$$(-96) \ \div \ (-12) \ = \ +8 \qquad (+56) \ \div \ (-7) \ = \ -8$$

The same rule applies to the division of decimals:

$$(+12.5932) \ \div \ (+3.6392) \ = \ +3.4604 \quad (-48.34) \ \div \ (-24.57) \ = \ +1.97$$

. . . and fractions:

$$\left(\frac{-33}{5}\right) \div \left(\frac{11}{25}\right) = \left(\frac{\overset{-3}{\cancel{-33}}}{\cancel{5}_{1}}\right) \cdot \left(\frac{\overset{5}{\cancel{25}}}{\cancel{11}_{1}}\right) = -15$$

$$\left(\frac{7}{3}\right) \div \left(\frac{-21}{9}\right) = \left(\frac{\overset{1}{7}}{\cancel{3}_{1}}\right) \cdot \left(\frac{\overset{3}{\cancel{9}}}{\cancel{-21}_{-3}}\right) = -1$$

Powers and Roots. When a number is multiplied by itself a certain number of times, we say that it is raised to that power. For example, if the number 2 if multiplied by itself 4 times, we say that it is raised to the fourth power:

$$\overset{\text{exponent}}{\underset{\text{base}}{2 \cdot 2 \cdot 2 \cdot 2 = 2^{4} = 16}}$$

In this example, 2 is called the *base* and 4 is called the *exponent.* Another way of saying this is "two to the fourth power." When the number 2 is multiplied by itself 4 times, the result is 16. Thus, we would say that, "two to the fourth power equals sixteen."

When an exponent is exactly divisible by 2, we say that it is an *even power.* For example, the exponents 2,4,6,8... are even powers. When an exponent is not exactly divisible by 2, we say that is is an *odd power.* For example, the exponents 1,3,5,7... are odd powers. A positive number raised to a positive exponent always yields a positive result. However, a negative number raised to an even power yields a positive result, and a negative number raised to an odd power yields a negative result. To help your child see this, consider the following examples:

$(-2)^1 = -2$ odd power yields negative result

$(-2)^2 = (-2)(-2) = +4$ even power yields positive result

$(-2)^3 = (-2)(-2)(-2) = -8$ odd power yields negative result

$(-2)^4 = (-2)(-2)(-2)(-2) = +16$ even power yields positive result

In the above examples, you should emphasize that $(-2)^2 \neq -2^2$, because $(-2)^2 = (-2)(-2) = +4$, and $-2^2 = -(2 \cdot 2) = -4$. You should also note that zero raised to any power is zero (e.g., $0^3 = 0 \cdot 0 \cdot 0 = 0$).

To help children understand the concept of a root, you can start off with the example of a *square root*. A square root of some number N is a number that, when multiplied by itself, equals N. For example:

$$2^2 = 2 \cdot 2 = 4 \qquad\qquad 3^2 = 3 \cdot 3 = 9$$

so the square root of 4 is 2   so the square root of 9 is 3

Another way to say this is $\sqrt{4} = 2$, and $\sqrt{9} = 3$. (The symbol used to indicate that the root is to be extracted from the number following it is called a radical sign.) Both of these square roots are called *principal square roots* because they are positive numbers. But note that both of these numbers also have negative square roots because $(-2) \cdot (-2) = 4$, and $(-3) \cdot (-3) = 9$. Thus, all positive numbers have both positive and negative square roots. The square root of a negative number is called an imaginary number, such as $\sqrt{-1}$, which will not be discussed here. Your child should not confuse this, however, with the square root of a positive number preceded by a negative sign, which is a straightforward calculation. For example:

$$-\sqrt{4} = -(2) = -2 \qquad -\sqrt{9} = -(3) = -3 \qquad -\sqrt{16} = -(4) = -4$$

When children are calculating the square root of a number, they can use trial and error to see if the square root is a whole number. If it is not, then they can find the answer by using either a square root table found in math books or a calculator if it has a square root key.

Numbers also have higher roots than square roots. For example, we can find the third (cube) root of the numbers 27 and -27 by inspection:

Since $3^3 = 3 \cdot 3 \cdot 3 = 27$, the cube root of 27 is 3.

Since $(-3)^3 = (-3) \cdot (-3) \cdot (-3) = -27$, the cube root of -27 is -3.

We write the cube root of a number by placing a 3 to the left of the radical sign, in the following way: $\sqrt[3]{27} = 3$, $\sqrt[3]{-27} = -3$. (Point out that we can take an odd root of a negative number, as we have done here, but we cannot take an even root of a negative number.) If we wanted to find a fourth root of a number, we would write a 4 to the left of the radical sign, and so on for higher roots. Your youngster can also find higher roots of a number using a calculator, if it is so equipped.

We can also have a higher root of a number preceded by a minus sign, as we saw above for square roots. For example:

$$-\sqrt[3]{27} = -(3) = -3 \qquad -\sqrt[3]{-27} = -(-3) = 3$$

A special case of higher roots involves the numbers 1 and -1. Any higher root of 1 is simply 1, because the number 1 multiplied by itself any number of times always equals 1:

$$1^3 = 1 \cdot 1 \cdot 1 = 1 \quad \text{so } \sqrt[3]{1} = 1 \qquad 1^4 = 1 \cdot 1 \cdot 1 \cdot 1 = 1 \quad \text{so } \sqrt[4]{1} = 1$$

We saw above that we cannot take $\sqrt{-1}$ because it is not defined on the real number line (it is an imaginary number). In other words, there is no real number that when multiplied by itself equals -1. We can, however, take $\sqrt[3]{-1}$, $\sqrt[5]{-1}$, and any other odd root of -1, which will always equal -1:

$$\text{Since } (-1)^3 = (-1) \cdot (-1) \cdot (-1) = -1, \sqrt[3]{-1} = -1$$

Emphasize to students that all of the roots that we have discussed here—both square and higher order roots—can be represented on the real number line.

Arithmetic Properties of Real Numbers

In the earlier chapter, Basic Arithmetic, you showed your child various arithmetic properties, such as the identity property, zero property, commutative property, associative property, and distributive property. We considered these properties for whole (non-negative) numbers, using actual numbers rather than symbols. We now want to reconsider these properties for all real numbers, with the use of algebraic symbols (a, b, and c below refer to any real numbers). In addition, we will introduce a new property called the inverse property. Since many of these properties are similar for addition and multiplication, they will be easier for your child to understand if we consider the two operations together in the discussion.

Identity Properties

The identity properties for addition and multiplication state that for any real number, we do not change its original value if we add 0 to the number or multiply it by 1:

	Addition	Multiplication
	$a + 0 = 0 + a = a$	$a \cdot 1 = 1 \cdot a = a$
let		
$a = 5$	$5 + 0 = 0 + 5 = 5$	$5 \cdot 1 = 1 \cdot 5 = 5$

In the above example, 0 is called the identity element for addition and 1 is called the identity element for multiplication. The multiplication identity will be very important later on when you show your youngster how to work with algebraic expressions involving fractions.

Operations with Zero

As we saw above, adding 0 to a number does not change its value. Subtracting 0 from any real number does not change its value, but subtracting a number from 0 gives its opposite:

	Subtracting 0 from a number	Subtracting a number from 0
	$a - 0 = a$	$0 - a = 0 + (-a) = -a$
let		
$a = -4$	$(-4) - 0 = -4$	$0 - (-4) = 0 + (+4) = 4$

Multiplication is nothing more than repeated addition of the same number, so multiplying a number by 0 yields a product of 0:

$$a \cdot 0 = 0 \cdot a = 0$$

let

$$a = 7 \qquad 7 \cdot 0 = 0 \cdot 7 = 0$$

As you showed your child in the earlier chapter on basic arithmetic, the number 0 can be divided by any number other than 0, but no number (including 0) can be divided by 0:

$\dfrac{0}{a} = 0$	$\dfrac{a}{0}$ is undefined	$\dfrac{0}{0}$ is undefined
let		
$a = 9 \quad \dfrac{0}{9} = 0$	$\dfrac{9}{0}$ is undefined	$\dfrac{0}{0}$ is undefined

Commutative Properties

The commutative property of addition says that if we change the order of numbers being added together, we get the same sum. The commutative property of multiplication says that if we change the order of numbers being multiplied together, we get the same product:

	Addition	Multiplication
let	$a + b = b + a$	$a \cdot b = b \cdot a$
$a = 3$		
$b = -7$	$3 + (-7) = (-7) + 3$	$(3) \cdot (-7) = (-7) \cdot (3)$

Associative Properties

The associative property of addition states that the sum of a set of numbers will be the same regardless of how we group them. The associative property of multiplication states that the product of a set of numbers will be the same regardless of how we group them:

let	Addition	Multiplication
$a = 2$	$(a + b) + c = a + (b + c)$	$(a \cdot b) \cdot c = a \cdot (b \cdot c)$
$b = -5$		
$c = 4$	$[2 + (-5)] + 4 = 2 + [(-5) + 4]$	$[2 \cdot (-5)] \cdot 4 = 2 \cdot [(-5) \cdot 4]$

Point out to your youngster that she can use brackets [ ] as well as parentheses ( ) to group numbers.

Distributive Property

The distributive property of multiplication over addition states that when a number is multiplied by an expression within a grouping symbol, the number must be multiplied by each term within the grouping symbol, and then the products are summed. This applies to any number of terms, but is illustrated below for three terms:

let	
$a = 6$	$a (b + c) = ab + ac$
$b = -2$	$6 [(-2) + 8] = 6 (-2) + 6 (8)$
$c = 8$	

Inverse Properties

When we add two numbers and the sum is 0, the numbers are called additive inverses. When we multiply two numbers and the product is 1, the numbers are called multiplicative inverses:

Addition	Multiplication
$a + (-a) = (-a) + a = 0$	$a \cdot \left(\dfrac{1}{a}\right) = \left(\dfrac{1}{a}\right) \cdot a = 1 \quad (a \neq 0)$
$-a$ is the additive inverse	$\dfrac{1}{a}$ is the multiplicative inverse

let

$a = 7 \quad 7 + (-7) = (-7) + 7 = 0 \qquad 7 \cdot \left(\dfrac{1}{7}\right) = \left(\dfrac{1}{7}\right) \cdot 7 = 1$

Order of Operations

In many algebraic expressions, one is required to perform more than one arithmetic operation. It is important to know the proper order of operations if you are to get the right answer. There are a few simple rules that will help you to perform operations in the right order:

Rule 1: If there are parentheses in an algebraic expression, always evaluate the part of the expression within the parentheses first.

Rule 2: When evalulating an algebraic expression, follow three steps in order:
    1. Evaluate powers and roots in any order.
    2. Perform multiplication and division in order from left to right.
    3. Perform addition and subtraction in order from left to right.

A good way for children to remember the proper order of operations is to learn the word PEMDAS, which stands for

Parentheses, Exponents, Multiplication, Division, Addition, and Subtraction.

Here is an example illustrating the proper order of operations:

$3\ (1+5)^2 - 4\sqrt{(7+9)}\ -\ 9$			Do the part inside parentheses first.
$=3\ (6)^2\qquad -4\ \ \sqrt{16}\qquad -\ 9$			Then take powers and roots.
$=3\,(36)\qquad -4\quad (4)\qquad -\ 9$			Then do multiplication from left to right.
$=\quad 108\qquad\ -16\qquad\qquad -\ 9$			Then do subtraction from left to right.
$=\quad 83$			This gives the final answer.

Symbols for grouping numbers together include:

Parentheses ( ) Brackets [ ] Braces { } Bar —— Square root $\sqrt{\ }$

These grouping symbols are used to change the normal order of operations within an algebraic expression. Operations are always performed within the grouping symbols before performing operations outside the grouping symbols. Parentheses, brackets, and braces all have the same meaning in an algebraic expression, and any combination of the above grouping symbols can be used in an expression. When several grouping symbols are present, we always do the part in the inside grouping symbols first. Here is an example:

$25 + 3\,\{2\,[(1+2)+3]\}^2$	Do the part inside parentheses first.
$=25+3\,\{2\,[\quad 3\quad +3]\}^2$	Do the part inside brackets next.
$=25+3\,\{2\cdot6\}^2$	Do the part inside braces next.
$=25+3\,\{12\}^2$	Take powers and roots next.
$=25+3\cdot144$	Then do multiplication from left to right.
$=25+432$	Then do addition from left to right.
$=457$	This gives the final answer.

One more example involving fractions (using the bar symbol) will be helpful to children:

$$16 + \frac{5 \cdot (1 + 2)^2}{4 \cdot (7 - 5)^2}$$ Do the part inside parentheses first, both above and beneath the bar.

$$= 16 + \frac{5 \cdot (3)^2}{4 \cdot (2)^2}$$ Take powers and roots next, both above and beneath the bar.

$$= 16 + \frac{5 \cdot 9}{4 \cdot 4}$$ Do multiplication from left to right, both above and beneath the bar.

$$= 16 + \frac{45}{16} = 18\frac{13}{16}$$ Do addition from left to right.

Evaluating Variable Expressions

In algebra we often use letters to represent numbers in expressions, such as x, y, and z. When the value of the letter can change in a problem, it is called a *variable*. In order to find the value of an algebraic expression that has both numbers and variables present, one should use the following rule:

Rule: First replace each variable in the equation with its numerical value, and then carry out all arithmetic operations using the proper order of operations described earlier.

As an example, find the value of the expression $4x^2 - 3xy - 4$, when $x = 3$ and $y = 6$:

$4 (3)^2 - 3 (3) (6) - 4$	Replace x and y with values. Take power first.
$= 4 (9) - 3 (3) (6) - 4$	Do multiplication from left to right.
$= 36 - 54 - 4$	Do subtraction from left to right.
$= 36 - 58 = -22$	This gives the final answer.

Some Basic Terminology

The above expression, $4x^2 - 3xy - 4$, is called an *algebraic expression* because it consists only of numbers, variables, arithmetic signs of operation, and grouping signs (although not all of these need to be present to have an algebraic expression). As we said earlier, a *variable* is a letter or symbol that can change its value in a given problem. For example, in the expression above, the letters x and y are variables. A *constant* is a number or symbol that cannot change its value in a given problem. For example, the numbers 4, 2, -3, and -4 are constants. As your child looks at the expression above, he can break it into smaller pieces separated by the arithmetic operations. By convention, each $+$ or $-$ is considered to be part of the term that follows it. For example, we would identify the terms in this expression as follows:

$4x^2$	$-3xy$	-4
First term	Second term	Third term

An exception to this rule is that everything within a grouping symbol is considered to be a single term, even though it may have plus signs and minus signs present. For example, the number of terms in the following expression is three:

$-15(2x + 3y)$	$+$	$\dfrac{4xz\,(2x + 7y)}{8xy\,(2x + 3y)}$	$+$	$4(2x + 3y)$
First term		Second term		Third term

Students need to become familiar with some terminology. Terms that have identical letters (often known as literal parts) are called like terms. Terms that do not have identical literal parts are called unlike terms. In the expression above, the first and third terms are like terms while the second term is not.

Now have your child take a closer look at the earlier expression we were discussing, $4x^2 - 3xy - 4$. We can see that the first term is the product of 4 and x^2. Numbers and letters that are multiplied together in a term are called *factors*. In this expression, 4 and x^2 are factors of the first term but not the second term; however, 4 is also a factor of the third term. Also point out that for all terms, the number 1 is also a factor, although it is usually not written. In the term $4x^2$, 4 is called the numerical coefficient and x^2 is called the literal coefficient. In common practice, however, the term *coefficient* is used to describe only the numerical coefficient. Thus, in the first term, 4 is the coefficient of x^2; in the second term, -3 is the coefficient of xy.

Polynomials

A *polynomial* in x is an algebraic expression that only has terms in the form of ax^n, where a is any real number, x is a variable, and n is a whole number. Because all of the terms in a polynomial are of the form ax^n, they do not have variables in the denominator. There are different names given to polynomials, depending upon the number of terms they have:

7x	is called a monomial because it has one term.
$3x^2 + 6x$	is called a binomial becuase it has two terms.
$4x^5 - 2x^3 + 9x$	is called a trinomial because it has three terms.

If a polynomial has more than three terms, it is generally not given a special name as in the above cases. Also, note that a number shown by itself, such as 7, technically can be considered a monomial because it equals $7 \cdot x^0 = 7 \cdot 1 = 7$. A polynomial in a single variable can be in any variable, such as a polynomial in y, a polynomial in z, and so forth.

Polynomials can have terms with more than one variable. For example, the expression we examined earlier, $4x^2 - 3xy$

− 4 is a polynomial in x and y because it only has terms in the form ax^ny^m, where a is any real number, x and y are variables, and n and m are whole numbers. A polynomial in two variables can have any two combinations of variables, such as x and y, u, and v, w, and z, and so forth. Here again, the polynomial is called a monomial if it has one term, binomial if it has two terms, and trinomial if it has three terms.

We can also talk about the *degree* of each of the terms in a polynomial and the degree of the polynomial itself. The degree of a term of a polynomial is the *sum* of the exponents of all of the variables in the term. For example, the degree of the following term is 5:

$3x^2y^2z$ has degree 5 because the sum of the exponents =
       $2 + 2 + 1 = 5$

The degree of the entire polynomial is the same as the degree of its highest term. The degree of the following polynomial in x is 4 because the degree of its highest term (term 1) is 4:

$$6x^4 \quad + \quad 7x^2 \quad + \quad 9$$
$$\text{degree 4} \qquad \text{degree 2} \qquad \text{degree 0}$$

Incidentally, notice that the terms of this polynomial are written in descending powers of the variable x, because the exponents get progressively smaller from the first to the last term. This is the way polynomials are usually expressed. If the polynomial was not in descending powers of x, its terms could be rearranged to look like the equation above.

Operations With Exponents

Earlier in the section on signed numbers, your youngster learned about the concepts of bases, exponents, and powers. We now want to broaden the discussion to include algebraic expressions with letters in them. If a variable x is multiplied by itself for a given number of times, we can write the variable with an exponent. For example, $x \cdot x \cdot x = x^3$. If we multiply two variables together that have the same base (say x), we might have the following situation.

$$x^2 \cdot x^4 = (x \cdot x) \cdot (x \cdot x \cdot x \cdot x) = x \cdot x \cdot x \cdot x \cdot x \cdot x = x^6$$

This suggests the following rule:

Rule: When multiplying two or more powers together that have the same base, we should add their exponents together.

let $\qquad\qquad\qquad x^a \cdot x^b = x^{a+b}$
$a = 3$
$b = 4$ $\qquad\qquad\qquad x^3 \cdot x^4 = x^{3+4} = x^7$

Note that the variables must have the same base for this rule to apply. If we wanted to multiply $x^2 y^3 z^4$, we could not add their exponents together because the bases are not the same.

Very often students will need to raise a power to another power. For example, suppose we want to raise x^3 to the second power, which is written as $(x^3)^2$. We could express this as follows:

$$(x^3)^2 = x^3 \cdot x^3 = x^{3+3} = x^6$$

This suggests the following rule:

Rule: When raising a power to another power, multiply the exponents together

let $\qquad\qquad\qquad (x^a)^b = x^{ab}$
$a = 2$
$b = 4$ $\qquad\qquad\qquad (x^2)^4 = x^{2 \cdot 4} = x^8$

Here again, note that the variables must have the same base for this rule to apply.

Your youngster will also have many occasions where he or she will need to divide one power by another. For example, consider the following expression:

$$\frac{x^6}{x^3} = \frac{x\,x\,x\,x\,x\,x}{x\,x\,x} = \frac{x\,x\,x \cdot x\,x\,x}{x\,x\,x \cdot 1} = 1 \cdot \frac{x\,x\,x}{1} = x\,x\,x = x^3$$

This suggests the following rule:

Rule: When dividing powers with the same base, subtract the exponent of the denominator from the exponent of the numerator (x must not be equal to 0, because this would involve division by 0).

$$\frac{x^a}{x^b} = x^{a-b}$$

let

$$a = 7$$
$$b = 4$$

$$\frac{x^7}{x^4} = x^{7-4} = x^3$$

The fact that we are subtracting the exponent of the denominator from the exponent of the numerator leads to the possibility that we may end up with a zero or negative exponent. Consider the following examples, in which the exponent of the numerator equals the exponent of the denominator:

$$\frac{x^3}{x^3} = \frac{x\,x\,x}{x\,x\,x} = 1 \quad \text{and} \quad \frac{x^3}{x^3} = x^{3-3} = x^0$$

These two examples together imply the following rule:

Rule: Any variable (or constant) raised to the power 0 equals 1. (The variable or constant must not be equal to 0 because this would imply division by 0.)

$$x^0 = 1 \quad (x \neq 0)$$

let

$$x = 5$$

$$5^0 = 1$$

Show your child the case in which the exponent of the denominator is larger than the exponent of the numerator.

$$\frac{x^2}{x^4} = \frac{x\,x}{x\,x\,x\,x} = \frac{1}{x^2} \quad \text{and} \quad \frac{x^2}{x^4} = x^{2-4} = x^{-2}$$

These two examples together imply the following rule:

Rule: Any variable (or constant) with a negative exponent can be represented by its multiplicative inverse (reciprocal). (The variable or constant must not be equal to 0 because this would imply division by 0.)

$$x^{-n} = \frac{1}{x^n} \qquad (x \neq 0)$$

let
$n = 2 \qquad x^{-2} = \frac{1}{x^2}$
$x = x$

let
$n = 2 \qquad 7^{-2} = \frac{1}{7^2}$
$x = 7$

Children should see that this implies that any factor can be moved from its numerator to its denominator, or vice versa, merely by changing the sign of its exponent. Point out that this only applies to factors (variables and constants being multiplied together) and will not work with variables or constants that are not factors. This operation does not change the sign of the overall expression. Here are some examples illustrating the concept:

$$y^{-n} = \frac{1}{y^n} \qquad y^n = \frac{1}{y^{-n}} \qquad \frac{a^{-2}b^{-2}c^{-2}}{x^{-1}y^{-1}z^{-1}} = \frac{xyz}{a^2b^2c^2}$$

$$\frac{a^3b^3c^3}{x^2y^2z^2} = a^3b^3c^3x^{-2}y^{-2}z^{-2}$$

The first and second examples illustrate that factors can be moved around, regardless of the sign of their exponents. The third example illustrates that an expression can be written without any negative exponents. The fourth example illustrates how an expression can be written without fractions.

All of the previous rules presented for positive exponents also apply with negative and zero exponents.

One final case involving exponents needs to be discussed, and that is the case in which an algebraic expression involving fractions is raised to some power. All of the rules we have discussed so far can be combined, resulting in the following rule:

Rule: When an expression involving fractions is raised to some power, say n, multiply that power by the exponents of all of the factors in the expression. (Here again, none of the variables or constants can have a value that will make the denominator equal to zero.)

let
a = 2
b = 3
c = 4
n = 2

$$\left(\frac{x^a}{y^b \ z^c}\right)^n = \frac{x^{an}}{y^{bn} \ z^{cn}}$$

$$\left(\frac{x^2}{y^3 \ z^4}\right)^2 = \frac{x^{2\cdot2}}{y^{3\cdot2} \ z^{4\cdot2}} = \frac{x^4}{y^6 \ z^8}$$

Simplifying a Product of Monomials

With these rules of exponents in mind, let's now return to our discussion of polynomials. In order to work with polynomials, we must be able to simplify a product of monomials. Here is a simple rule that will enable us to do this:

Rule: To simplify a product of monomials, you must follow three steps:

Step 1: First write the sign of the product. The sign is positive if there are no negative factors or if there is an even number of negative factors. The sign is negative if there is an odd number of negative factors.

Step 2: Next write the number of the product. To do this, multiply the absolute values of all of the numbers together.

Step 3: Then find the letters of the product. Use the rules of exponents to find the exponent of each letter in the product. Then arrange the letters in alphabetical order.

You can use the following example to illustrate the application of this rule. Simplify the following product of monomials:

$(-3x^2y)(-2xz^4)(-3y^3z)$

$= -(3 \cdot 2 \cdot 3)(x^2x)(yy^3)(z^4z)$ Use the associative property to regroup; commutative property to change order.

$= -(18)(x^3)(y^4)(z^5)$ Variables combined using rule of exponents. Absolute values of numbers multiplied out. Odd number of negative factors.

$= -18x^3y^4z^5$

Removing Grouping Symbols

When removing grouping symbols, such as parentheses, we simply remove the symbols if they are preceeded by a plus sign (or no sign) and do not change the sign of the terms inside the grouping symbols. As an example:

$$(4x + 3y) + (5x - 2y) = 4x + 3y + 5x - 2y$$

If grouping symbols are preceded by a minus sign, we drop the minus sign and change the sign of each enclosed term when the grouping symbols are removed. Here is an example:

$$(3x - 7y) - (6x - 9y) = 3x - 7y - 6x + 9y$$

When grouping symbols are preceded by a factor, we must multiply each enclosed term by the factor when removing the grouping symbols. (This is an application of the distributive property.)

$$-4x\,(3x\,-\,5)\,=\,-4x\,(3x)\,+\,(-4x)\,(-5)\,=\,-12x^2\,+\,20x$$

When removing grouping symbols that are inside of other grouping symbols, we should remove the innermost grouping symbols first. As an example:

$$w\,-\,[x\,-\,(y\,-\,z)]\,=\,w\,-\,[x\,-\,y\,+\,z]\,=\,w\,-\,x\,+\,y\,-\,z$$

Combining Like Terms

When combining like terms, we first need to identify like terms (those with the same letters or literal parts) and then sum each group of like terms. To do this, we must add their numerical coefficients and then multiply this sum by the literal parts of the like terms. To illustrate:

$$2x\,-\,6x\,+\,7y\,+\,4y\,=\,(2\,-\,6)\,x\,+\,(7\,+\,4)\,y\,=\,-4x\,+\,11y$$

Here is another example that requires regrouping the like terms before combining them:

$$6x^2\,+\,3x\,-\,4\,-\,2x^2\,+\,7x\,+\,3$$
$$=\,6x^2\,-\,2x^2\,+\,3x\,+\,7x\,-\,4\,+\,3$$
$$=\,(6\,-\,2)\,x^2\,+\,(3\,+\,7)\,x\,+\,(-4\,+\,3)$$
$$=\,4x^2\,+\,10x\,-\,1$$

Addition of Polynomials

To add polynomials, all you need to do is show your child how to follow the above two operations, in order: (1) remove the grouping symbols, and (2) combine like terms. Here is an example:

$$(4x - 7y) + (5x + 9y)$$ This is the original expression.
$$= 4x - 7y + 5x + 9y$$ Remove the grouping symbols.
$$= 4x + 5x - 7y + 9y$$ Combine like terms.
$$= (4 + 5) x + (-7 + 9) y$$ Multiply the sum of numerical
$$= 9x + 2y$$ coefficients by their literal parts.

Here is another example showing how to add polynomials by removing the grouping symbols and combining like terms:

$$(7x^2y - 6xy^2) + (5xy - 2x^2y) + (8xy^2 - 9xy)$$
$$= 7x^2y - 6xy^2 + 5xy - 2x^2y + 8xy^2 - 9xy$$
$$= 7x^2y - 2x^2y - 6xy^2 + 8xy^2 + 5xy - 9xy$$
$$= (7 - 2) x^2y + (-6 + 8) xy^2 + (5 - 9) xy$$
$$= 5x^2y + 2xy^2 - 4xy$$

Sometimes it is more convenient to add polynomials vertically. To do this, arrange the polynomials one under another so the like terms are in the same vertical line. Then find the sum of all of the terms in a line by adding their numerical coefficients together. Here is an example illustrating the approach. Add the following polynomials together vertically:

$$(3x^3 + 4x - 5), (x^2 - 2x + 9), \text{ and } (2x^3 - 7x^2 - 3).$$

$$
\begin{array}{r}
3x^3 \phantom{{}- 7x^2} + 4x - 5 \\
x^2 - 2x + 9 \\
+\,2x^3 - 7x^2 \phantom{{}+ 2x} - 3 \\
\hline
5x^3 - 6x^2 + 2x + 1 \\
\end{array}
$$

Subtraction of Polynomials

Subtraction of polynomials is very similar to addition of polynomials, so it should be easy for your youngster to comprehend. As with signed numbers, first we change the sign of the polynomials being subtracted, and then we proceed as in the addition of polynomials. As an example:

$(4x - 8y) - (2x + 6y)$	This is the original expression.
$= 4x - 8y - 2x - 6y$	Remove the grouping symbols and change the signs of terms being subtracted.
$= 4x - 2x - 8y - 6y$	Combine like terms.
$= (4 - 2) x + (-8 - 6) y$	Multiply the sum of numerical
$= 2x - 14y$	coefficients by their literal parts.

Here is another example illustrating the subtraction of polynomials when two sets of grouping symbols are present:

$(6x + 9) - [(4x - 7) - (2x + 3)]$	This is the original expression.
$= (6x + 9) - [4x - 7 - 2x - 3]$	Remove the innermost parentheses, and change signs of subtracted numbers.
$= 6x + 9 - 4x + 7 + 2x + 3$	Remove parentheses and brackets, and change signs of subtracted numbers.
$= 6x - 4x + 2x + 9 + 7 + 3$	Combine like terms.
$= (6 - 4 + 2) x + (9 + 7 + 3)$	Multiply the sum of numerical
$= 4x + 19$	coefficients by their literal parts.

Again, it may be more convenient for your child to subtract polynomials vertically, in a manner similar to the way they are added vertically. All she needs to do is change the signs of the terms being subtracted, and then proceed as in addition. For example, suppose she wants to subtract $(4x^3 + 2x - 5)$ from $(10x^3 - 3x^2 + 7x + 6)$:

$$
\begin{array}{r}
10x^3 - 3x^2 + 7x + 6 \\
+ -\ 4x^3 \qquad\quad -\ 2x + 5 \\
\hline
6x^3 - 3x^2 + 5x + 11
\end{array}
$$

Change the signs of the terms being subtracted, and then proceed as in addition.

Multiplication of Polynomials

The multiplication of polynomials basically involves the repeated application and extension of the distributive property that we discussed earlier:

$$w(x + y + z) = wx + wy + wz \qquad (x + y + z)w = xw + yw + zw$$

Thus, to multiply a polynomial by a monomial, we simply multiply each term in the polynomial by the monomial, and then add the results together. Here is an example:

$$-7x(5x^3 - 4x^2 + 9x - 6)$$
$$= (-7x)(5x^3) + (-7x)(-4x^2) + (-7x)(9x) + (-7x)(-6)$$
$$= \quad -35x^4 \qquad +28x^3 \qquad -63x^2 \qquad +42x$$

To multiply two polynomials together, we need to multiply the first polynomial by each term in the second polynomial and then add the results together. This requires us to apply the distributive property twice. For example, here is how we multiply $(3x + 4)$ by $(2x - 6)$:

$(3x + 4)(2x - 6)$	Original expression
$= (3x + 4)(2x) + (3x + 4)(-6)$	Distributive property
$= (3x)(2x) + (4)(2x) + (3x)(-6) + (4)(-6)$	Distributive property
$= 6x^2 + 8x - 18x - 24$	Multiply expression
$= 6x^2 - 10x - 24$	Combine like terms

Another way to show your child how to multiply two polynomials together is to arrange them in the same way we would use for multiplying two whole numbers together. This approach is particularly useful when the polynomials have multiple terms. For example, to multiply $(4x^3 - 2x^2 + 6x - 3)$ by $(5x - 7)$:

$$
\begin{array}{r}
4x^3 \; - 2x^2 \; + 6x \; - 3 \\
5x \; - 7 \\
\hline
-28x^3 + 14x^2 - 42x + 21 \\
+20x^4 - 10x^3 + 30x^2 - 15x \\
\hline
+20x^4 - 38x^3 + 44x^2 - 57x + 21
\end{array}
$$

When a polynomial is raised to a power, we can find the result by repeated multiplications of the polynomial. For example, if we want to find $(x - y)^3$, we can set this up as a multiplication problem in which we perform two successive multiplications:

First multiply $(x - y)$ by $(x - y)$, then multiply $x^2 - 2xy + y^2$ by $(x - y)$

$$
\begin{array}{r}
x - y \\
x - y \\
\hline
- xy + y^2 \\
x^2 - xy \\
\hline
x^2 - 2xy + y^2
\end{array}
\qquad
\begin{array}{r}
x^2 - 2xy + y^2 \\
x - y \\
\hline
- x^2y + 2xy^2 - y^3 \\
x^3 - 2x^2y + xy^2 \\
\hline
x^3 - 3x^2y + 3xy^2 - y^3
\end{array}
$$

Division of Polynomials

To divide a polynomial by a monomial, we need to divide each individual term of the polynomial by the monomial and then add the results together. For example:

$$\frac{15x^3 - 9x^2 + 6x}{-3x} = \frac{15x^3}{-3x} + \frac{-9x^2}{-3x} + \frac{6x}{-3x} = -5x^2 + 3x - 2$$

If the polynomial and monomial consist of multiple literal parts, the division is performed in the same manner:

$$\frac{16x^2y - 12xz^2 + 8y^2z}{-4xy} = \frac{16x^2y}{-4xy} + \frac{-12xz^2}{-4xy} + \frac{+8y^2z}{-4xy}$$

$$= -4x + \frac{3z^2}{y} - \frac{2yz}{x}$$

To divide one polynomial by another, your youngster can use an approach similar to long division with whole numbers. Suppose, for example, that we want to divide $(x^2 - 7x + 12)$ by $(x - 3)$:

$$
\begin{array}{r}
x - 4 \\
x - 3 \overline{)\, x^2 - 7x + 12\,} \\
\underline{x^2 - 3x} \\
-4x + 12 \\
\underline{-4x + 12} \\
0
\end{array}
$$

The first term in the quotient (x) is equal to the first term in the dividend (x^2) divided by the first term in the divisor (x).

Subtract ($x^2 - 3x$) from ($x^2 - 7x$).

Subtract ($-4x + 12$) from ($-4x + 12$).

Sometimes when dividing polynomials, it is necessary to add spaces for missing powers of terms. Suppose, for example, that we wanted to divide ($y^3 - 1$) by ($y - 1$):

$$
\begin{array}{r}
y^2 + y + 1 \\
y - 1 \overline{)\, y^3 + 0y^2 + 0y - 1\,} \\
\underline{y^3 - y^2} \\
y^2 + 0y \\
\underline{y^2 - y} \\
y - 1 \\
\underline{y - 1} \\
0
\end{array}
$$

The terms $0y^2$ and $0y$ have been added to the dividend to make it easier to line up the terms when performing the division.

When dividing polynomials, the terms in the dividend and divisor should always be ordered in descending powers of the variable (y in this problem), before making the division.

Solving Equations

In order to solve problems, your child will need to know how to solve equations. In this section we will concentrate on solving first-degree equations with one unknown value. First, we will review some basic concepts about equations. An equation has three parts: the left side, the equal sign, and the right side. For example, consider the following equation:

$$4x + 8 = 7x + 2$$

What this equation says is that the quantity on the left side is the same as the quantity on the right side. To solve this equation your child must find the unknown number x, which when substituted into the equation makes the left side equal to the right side. To do this, she needs to get the unknown value of x on one side of the equation and a single number on the other side. (It doesn't matter which side of the equation the unknown value of x is on.) In manipulating the numbers and letters to accomplish this, one rule is very important:

Rule: If we perform the same arithmetic operation on both sides of the equation, the value of the equation stays the same.

This rule says we have not changed the value of the equation if we add the same number to both sides of the equation, subtract the same number from both sides of the equation, multiply both sides of the equation by the same number, or divide both sides of the equation by the same number. Now you can use the rule to solve equations for each of these cases.

Suppose we want to solve the equation: $x - 7 = 10$. If we add 7 to both sides of the equation, the value of the equation will not change. This will leave x on one side of the equation and a single number on the other side, enabling us to solve for x:

$x - 7 =$	10	This is the original expression.	
$+ 7$	$+ 7$	Add 7 to both sides of the equation.	
$x \quad =$	17	This enables us to solve for x.	

Now suppose your child wants to solve the equation: $-11 = x + 4$. If he subtracts 4 from both sides of the equation, the value of the equation will not change. This will leave x on one side of the equation and a single number on the other side, enabling him to solve for x:

$$-11 = x + 4$$ This is the original expression.

$$\underline{-4 \qquad -4}$$ Subtract 4 from both sides of the equation.

$$-15 = x$$ This enables us to solve for x.

Point out that x is on the right side of the equation here and on the left side of the equation in the previous example. It doesn't matter which side of the equation x appears on. The statements $-15 = x$ and $x = -15$ are equivalent statements.

As another example, suppose he wants to solve the equation: $\dfrac{x}{6} = 5$. If he multiplies each side of the equation by 6, this will not change the value of the equation. This will leave x on one side of the equation and a single number on the other side, allowing us to solve for x:

$$\frac{x}{6} = 5$$ This is the original expression.

$$6\left(\frac{x}{6}\right) = 6(5)$$ Multiply each side by 6.

$$x = 30$$ This enables us to solve for x.

Now suppose that he wants to solve the equation: $28 = 4x$. If he divides each side of the equation by 4, this will not change the value of the equation. This will leave x on one side of the equation and a single number on the other side, which allows him to solve for x:

$$28 = 4x$$ This is the original expression.

$$\frac{28}{4} = \frac{4x}{4}$$ Divide each side by 4.

$$7 = x$$ This is the solution.

Emphasize to students that it is always a good idea to check our solutions to equations to make sure that we have performed our calculations correctly. To do this, we replace the unknown letter in the equation with the number we obtained as a solution. We then perform the operations indicated on both sides of the equal sign, and if both sides are equal then the solution is correct. Let's apply this approach to the equation we just solved:

Solution.   Check for the solution.

$28 = 4x$	$28 = 4x$	This is the original expression.
$\dfrac{28}{4} = \dfrac{4x}{4}$	$28 = 4(7)$	Replace x with 7 (the solution).
$7 = x$	$28 = 28$	Both sides equal each other, so the solution is correct.

Here is another example involving fractions: $\dfrac{4x}{5} = 16$. In this example we can either divide both sides of the equation by $\dfrac{4}{5}$ or multiply both sides by $\dfrac{5}{4}$; either approach will not change the value of the equation. Let's try the latter approach and check our solution:

Solution.	Check for the solution.
$\dfrac{4x}{5} = 16$	$\dfrac{4x}{5} = 16$
$\dfrac{5}{4}\left(\dfrac{4x}{5}\right) = \dfrac{5}{4}(16)$	$\dfrac{4\,(20)}{5} = 16$
$x = 20$	$16 = 16$

Solving More Complicated Equations

Many equations are more complicated than the ones we examined in the previous section. Often it is necessary to simplify the terms in an equation to find a solution. The methods of doing this are basically the same as the ones we have already discussed, although sometimes we have to group like terms and then apply the methods several times.

Here is a description of the process you can give to your youngster: First we should remove the grouping symbols and then combine like terms on each side of the equation. Then we should move the unknown value to one side of the equation and all of the numbers to the other side of the equation. In doing this, we should use the addition or subtraction rule first, and then the multiplication or division rule next. It is always a good idea to check our solution to the problem to make sure that we have performed our calculations correctly. Let's do a few examples to illustrate the approach:

To solve the equation, $8x + 5 = 29$, we first have to subtract 5 from each side before dividing by 8, in order to get x on one side of the equation and one number on the other side of the equation:

Solution.		Check.

$$
\begin{array}{rcl}
8x + 5 &=& 29 \\
-5 && -5 \\
\hline
\dfrac{8x}{8} &=& \dfrac{24}{8} \\
x &=& 3
\end{array}
$$

Original expression.	$8x + 5 = 29$
Subtract 5 from each side.	$8\,(3) + 5 = 29$
Divide each side by 8.	$24 + 5 = 29$
This is the solution.	$29 = 29$

Sometimes the unknown value occurs on both sides of the equal sign, and we need to combine like terms before carrying out the other steps to solve the equation. As an example, suppose we want to solve the equation, $4x + 12 = -2x - 6$:

Solution.		Check.

$$
\begin{array}{rcl}
4x + 12 &=& -2x - 6 \\
+2x && +2x \\
\hline
6x + 12 &=& -6 \\
-12 && -12 \\
\hline
\dfrac{6x}{6} &=& -\dfrac{18}{6} \\
x &=& -3
\end{array}
$$

Original expression.	$4x + 12 = -2x - 6$
Add 2x to each side.	$4\,(-3) + 12 = -2\,(-3) - 6$
Subtract 12 from each side.	$-12 + 12 = +6 - 6$
	$0 = 0$
Divide each side by 6.	
This is the solution.	

Here is one more example that requires the removal of grouping symbols before combining like terms and carrying out the other steps to solve an equation:

$4[-(x-2)+3] =$	$6(x-1)+16$	Original expression.
$4[-x+2+3] =$	$6x-6+16$	
$4[-x+5] =$	$6x+10$	Remove grouping symbols.
$-4x+20 =$	$6x+10$	
$+4x$	$+4x$	Add 4x to each side.
$20 =$	$10x+10$	
-10	-10	Subtract 10 from each side.
$\dfrac{10}{10} =$	$\dfrac{10x}{10}$	Divide each side by 10.
$1 = x$		This is the solution.

Check.

$4[-(x-2)+3] = 6(x-1)+16$	Original expression.
$4[-(1-2)+3] = 6(1-1)+16$	Substitute 1 for x.
$4[-(-1)+3] = 6(0)+16$	
$4[1+3] = 16$	Remove grouping symbols.
$4[4] = 16$	
$16 = 16$	The solution is correct.

The above equation, and all of the equations you have shown your child so far, are true for only certain values of the unknown number. For example, both sides of the above equation are equal to each other only if x equals 1. The two sides will not equal each other for any other value of x. Equations that have solutions for only certain values are known as *conditional equations.*

In some equations, both sides are equal to each other regardless of the value that is substituted for x. Such equations, which are known as *identities*, have an infinite number of solutions. You can always recognize identities because, after doing some arithmetic, both sides reduce down to the same thing. Here is an example:

$40x-16 = 4(10x-4)$	This is an identity because both sides
$40x-16 = 40x-16$	reduce to the same expression. This equation is true for any value of x.

Students should also know that there are some equations in which both sides will not be equal for any value of x. Such equations have no solution. Here is an example:

$$5x + 4 = 5x - 3$$
$$\underline{-5x \qquad\quad -5x}$$
$$4 = -3$$

This equation has no solution, because if we subtract 5x from both sides, we can see that 4 is not equal to -3.

All of the equations we have discussed so far have been one equation with one unknown. We have been able to solve these equations as long as they are conditional equations. If one equation has more than one unknown value, we can only solve for one unknown in terms of the other unknown values. Such equations are called *literal equations*. For example, if we are asked to solve the equation $x - 3y = 8$ for x, the solution would be as follows:

$$x - 3y = 8$$
$$\underline{+ 3y \qquad\quad + 3y}$$
$$x \qquad = 8 + 3y$$

Notice that while we are able to get x on one side of the equation, the other side contains the value y and numbers.

Solving Inequalities

Your child will also be required to solve inequalities. Inequalities are different from equations in one major respect. An equation says that the left side equals ($=$) the right side. An inequality says that the left side does not equal the right side. There are several different forms that an inequality can take:

If we say that x is not equal to ($\neq$) y, we would write this as follows:

$$x \neq y \qquad \text{For example, } 5 \neq 3.$$

Another form of an inequality is to say that x is greater than ($>$) y:

$$x > y \qquad \text{For example, } 9 > 7.$$

As a variation of this, we might say that x is greater than or equal to (≥) y. This means that either x is greater than y or x is equal to y:

$$x \geq y \qquad \text{Examples are } 9 \geq 7 \text{ and } 4 \geq 4.$$

In contrast, if x is less than (<) y, we would write this as follows:

$$x < y \qquad \text{For example, } 6 < 8.$$

As a variation of this, we might say that x is less than or equal to (≤) y. This means that either x is less than y or x is equal to y:

$$x \leq y \qquad \text{Examples are } 6 \leq 8 \text{ and } 2 \leq 2.$$

You should be aware that different inequality symbols can be used to say the same thing. For example, $5 > 3$ is the same as saying that $3 < 5$.

Both unknown values and numbers frequently occur together in inequalities. For example, consider the following inequalities:

$$2x + 3 < 11 \qquad 6(x - 3) \geq 2x - 22 \qquad -8x + 4 \leq -12$$

Explain to your child that to solve an inequality means to get the unknown letter on one side of the inequality symbol and everything else on the other side. The rules for solving inequalities are very similar to the rules for solving equations, with a few exceptions. We can add and subtract the same number to both sides of the inequality without changing its value. We can also multiply and divide both sides of the inequality by the same number, *as long as the number is positive*. If we multiply or divide both sides of the inequality by a negative number, we must reverse the direction—or *sense*—of the inequality symbol. For example, if we multiply or divide both sides of an inequality by a negative number and the inequality symbol is "greater than," we must change it to "less than." Let's now apply these rules to solve the inequalities shown above:

$$2x + 3 < 11$$ This is the original inequality.
$$\underline{-3 \quad -3}$$ Subtract 3 from both sides.
$$\frac{2x}{2} < \frac{8}{2}$$ Divide both sides by 2.
$$x < 4$$ The solution is x is less than 4.

Notice that the direction (or sense) of the inequality symbol did not change with these calculations because we divided both sides by a positive number $(+2)$ and not a negative number.

Children can gain a better understanding of what this inequality says by graphing it on a number line:

Notice the hollow circle around 4 because it is not a solution.

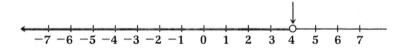

As shown by the arrow, all numbers to the left of 4 are part of the solution.

Now let's tackle the next inequality:

$$6(x - 3) \geq 2x - 22$$ This is the original inequality.
$$6x - 18 \geq 2x - 22$$ Remove the grouping symbols.
$$\underline{-2x \qquad -2x}$$ Subtract 2x from each side.
$$4x - 18 \geq -22$$
$$\underline{+18 \qquad +18}$$ Add 18 to each side.
$$\frac{4x}{4} \geq -\frac{4}{4}$$ Divide each side by 4.
$$x \geq -1$$ The solution is x is greater than or equal to -1.

Here again, the sense of the inequality symbol did not change, because we divided both sides by a positive number ($+4$) and not a negative number. As in the previous example, we can also graph this inequality on a number line:

Notice the solid circle around -1 because it is a solution.

As shown by the arrow, -1 and all numbers to the right of -1 are a solution.

The third inequality we used as an example requires division by a negative number, which reverses the sense of the inequality:

$-8x + 4 \leq -12$	This is the original inequality.
$\underline{-4 \quad -4}$	Subtract 4 from each side.
$\dfrac{-8x}{-8} \leq \dfrac{-16}{-8}$	Divide each side by -8.
$x \geq 2$	The solution is x is greater than or equal to 2.

Emphasize to your child that, in contrast to the two previous examples, the sense of the inequality symbol reverses in the last step because we have divided both sides by a negative number (-8). As noted earlier, if we had multiplied both sides by a negative number (say $-\dfrac{1}{8}$), this also would have reversed the sense of the inequality symbol.

The graph of this inequality reflects the reversed inequality symbol:

Notice the solid circle around 2 because it is a solution.

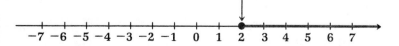

As shown by the arrow, 2 and all numbers to the right of 2 are a solution.

Solving Word Problems

Algebra is a very useful subject because it can solve a variety of practical problems. Many of these problems are stated in words, commonly known as word problems. Students often have difficulty with word problems because they do not know how to translate the words into algebraic expressions. The first step in solving word problems is knowing how to break statements into smaller expressions. Here is an example of some common statements and how they are translated into algebraic expressions:

Common Statements	Algebraic Expressions
The sum of some number and 4.	$x + 4$
7 more than some number.	$x + 7$
Some number is added to 5.	$5 + x$
Some number is increased by 1.	$x + 1$
Some number is decreased by 1.	$x - 1$
The difference between some number and 2.	$x - 2$
9 is subtracted from some number.	$x - 9$
6 less than some number.	$x - 6$
Some number is multiplied by 5.	$5x$
The product of some number and 10.	$10x$
3 times some number.	$3x$
Some number is divided by 2.	$\dfrac{x}{2}$
The quotient of some number and 14.	$\dfrac{x}{14}$

Now that your student is familiar with how to change a word phrase into an algebraic expression, we can expand this to include the translation of a word problem into an algebraic expression. To do this, we first need to identify the number or numbers that are unknown, then represent the number or numbers in terms of the same letter, and then finally write the expression as an equation or inequality using the letter rather than the unknown numbers. We can then solve the equation or inequality, and check our solution to make sure that it is accurate. Here is an example you can show to your youngster. Suppose that the sum of two unknown numbers is 16, and the second number is 8 more than the first number. What are the two numbers?

Let x be the first number, and x + 8 be the second number. Then:

x + (x + 8) = 16,	so	2x + 8 = 16	Combine x.
first number second number		$\underline{-8\quad -8}$	Subtract 8.
The first number x = 4.		$\dfrac{2x}{2} = \dfrac{8}{2}$	Divide by 2.
The second number (x + 8) = 12.		x = 4	
And 4 + 12 = 16. (Solution is correct.)			

Now you can show your child how to do another example that is a little more complicated. Suppose that six times an unknown number is six more than three times the sum of the number and 2. What is the unknown number? In such cases, we should break the problem down into small pieces and then represent each piece with an algebraic expression. This makes the problem much easier to solve. Let's do the problem:

Six times a number is six more than three times the sum of the number and 2.

6 · x = 6 + 3 · (x + 2)	
6x = 6 + 3 (x + 2)	
6x = 6 + 3x + 6	Remove the grouping symbols.
3x = 12	Subtract 3x from each side and combine the 6's.
x = 4	Divide each side by 3.

The unknown number is 4. To check this solution, plug 4 back into the original equation and make sure that both sides are equal:

$$6x = 6 + 3 (x + 2)$$
$$6(4) = 6 + 3 (4 + 2) \qquad \text{Substitute 4 for x.}$$
$$24 = 24 \qquad \text{The solution checks out.}$$

In an earlier chapter your student learned about ratios, proportions, and percents. Many word problems involving these concepts require the use of algebra for a solution.

Let's do an example involving a *ratio*. Suppose that two numbers have a ratio of 3 to 8 and their sum is 33. What are the two numbers? To solve a problem like this, we should multiply each term of the ratio by some letter (say, x) to represent the unknown values:

$$3x + 8x = 33 \qquad \text{Multiply each term of the ratio by x and set sum} = 33$$
$$11x = 33 \qquad \text{Combine the unknown values.}$$
$$x = 3 \qquad \text{Divide each side by 11.}$$

Check:

$3x = 3 (3) = 9$ This is the smaller number. $\dfrac{9}{24} = \dfrac{3}{8}$ and $9 + 24$

$8x = 8 (3) = 24$ This is the larger number. $\phantom{\dfrac{9}{24} = \dfrac{3}{8} and } = 33$

From an earlier chapter, you should remember that a proportion says that two ratios are equal. As an example of a *proportion* problem, if a building 100 feet high casts a shadow 80 feet long, how long will the shadow be for a building that is 250 feet high? Here, the unknown value (say, x) is the length of the shadow for a building 250 feet high. We can solve for x by setting the problem up as a proportion (note that the length of the shadow is the numerator of both ratios):

shadow for 100 ft bldg	$\dfrac{80}{100} = \dfrac{x}{250}$	shadow for 250 ft bldg
100 ft bldg		250 ft bldg
cross-multiply	$(250)\,80 = x\,(100)$	cross-multiply
divide by 100	$(250)\,(.8) = x$	divide by 100
	$200 \text{ feet} = x$	shadow for 250 ft bldg

Thus, the length of a shadow projected by a building 250 feet high is 200 feet. As a check, if we replace x by 200, we see that both sides of the proportion equal .8:

$$.8 = \frac{80}{100} = \frac{200}{250} = .8$$

Another common type of word problem students will encounter involves *percents*. The approach for solving percent word problems is very similar to what we have done already. We first represent the unknown value by a letter and then translate the word problem into an algebraic expression. The main difference is that we need to convert all percents to decimals before carrying out the calculations. If the unknown value we are trying to find is a percent, we need to convert the decimal representation back to a percent to get the right answer. Suppose that we have to pay a 4 percent sales tax on all purchases of goods. If we buy a stereo set that costs $300, how much should we expect to pay in sales taxes?

Let x equal the unknown amount we have to pay in sales taxes.

x = 4% of 300	Set up the problem as 4 percent of $300.
x = .04 (300)	Convert 4 percent to a decimal and multiply by 300.
x = 12	The amount of sales tax we have to pay is $12.

Alternatively, the problem might have been set up as follows. If we had to pay $12 sales tax on a $300 stereo, what percent of sales tax did we have to pay?

Let x equal the unknown percent of sales tax that we have to pay.

12 = x (300)	Translate the word problem into an algebraic expression
$\dfrac{12}{300} = \dfrac{x\ (300)}{300}$	Divide both sides of the equation by 300.
.04 = x	Solve for the unknown value of x.
4% = x	Convert the decimal representation to a percent. The percent of sales tax we have to pay is 4%.

A related group of word problems concern *variation*. In this type of problem we have two variables that are related to each other through multiplication or division. For example, the variables x and y might vary as described by the formula $y = kx$. This says that y, which is called the dependent variable, varies in direct proportion to x, which is called the independent variable. The value k is called the constant of proportionality and describes how y is related to x. If x goes up or down by a certain amount, then y goes up or down by the amount kx. If we know the values of x and y, we can solve for k. For example, suppose that y varies directly with x, and y equals 18 when x equals 6. Solve for the value of k:

$y = k \cdot x$ This is the variation formula.

$18 = k \cdot 6$ Substitute for the values of x and y.

$\dfrac{18}{6} = \dfrac{k \cdot 6}{6}$ Divide each side of the equation by 6 to solve for k.

$3 = k$ Simplify. The constant of proportionality is 3.

Now that your child knows the constant of proportionality, she can determine what y will be for any given value of x. For example, suppose she wants to find the value of y when x equals 4, given that the constant of proportionality is 3. Here is how she would solve the problem:

$y = k \cdot x$ This is the variation formula.

$y = 3 \cdot x$ Substitute the value of 3 for k.

$y = 3 \cdot 4$ Substitute the value of 4 for x, which is given.

$y = 12$ This shows that y equals 12 when x equals 4.

Sometimes the variables x and y will vary inversely with each other. The variation formula for these types of problems is $y = \dfrac{k}{x}$. Again, y is the dependent variable, x is the independent variable, and k is the constant of proportionality. This says that as x gets larger, y gets smaller; alternatively, as x gets smaller, y gets larger. Your child can use the same methods to solve inverse variation problems that she used for direct variation problems. For example, if y equals 4 and x equals 6, find the value of k:

$$y = \frac{k}{x}$$ This is the variation formula.

$$4 = \frac{k}{6}$$ Substitute the values for x and y.

$$4\,(6) = \frac{k\,(6)}{6}$$ Multiply each side of the equation by 6.

$$24 = k$$ The constant of proportionality equals 24.

As with the previous example, once your youngster knows the constant of proportionality, he can solve for one variable given the value of the other variable. For example, suppose that he wants to find the value of y when x equals 8, given that the constant of proportionality is 24:

$$y = \frac{k}{x}$$ This is the variation formula.

$$y = \frac{24}{x}$$ Substitute the value of 24 for k.

$$y = \frac{24}{8}$$ Substitute the value of 8 for x, which is given.

$$y = 3$$ This shows that y equals 3 when x equals 8.

One final type of word problem students should know about is the *mixture* problem, in which two quantities of something are combined to equal a total amount. For example, if I tell you that I have 13 coins that equal $2.05, and they are all nickels and quarters, I may want you to figure out how many nickels and quarters I have. The secret to solving a problem like this is to define one coin in terms of the other coin, and then multiply these quantities by the value of the coins to get the total amount. Here is how it is done:

If N equals the number of nickels, then $13 - N$ equals the number of quarters because the total number of coins equals 13. Now multiply the value of each coin times the number of coins and set the sum equal to 13:

(value of a nickel) (# nickels) + (value of a quarter) (# quarters) = (total)

$$(.05) \quad \cdot \quad (N) \quad + \quad (.25) \quad \cdot \quad (13 - N) \quad = \quad 2.05$$

$.05\,N + .25\,(13 - N) = 2.05$	
$5\,N + 25\,(13 - N) = 205$	Multiply each side of the equation by 10.
$5\,N + 325 - 25\,N = 205$	Remove the grouping symbols.
$-20\,N = -120$	Combine N and subtract 325 from each side.
$N = 6$	Divide each side by -20.

Thus, the number of nickels (N) = 6. The number of quarters $(13 - N)$ = 7. We can check our result in the following manner:

$$
\begin{aligned}
6 \text{ nickels} &= 6\,(5) = 30\text{¢} \\
7 \text{ quarters} &= 7\,(25) = 175\text{¢} \\
13 \text{ coins} & = 205\text{¢} = \$2.05
\end{aligned}
$$

Summary

In this first chapter on algebra we have covered a variety of topics. We discussed basic concepts such as natural numbers, whole numbers, and negative numbers. We introduced the concept of a number line and noted that rational and irrational numbers make up the set of real numbers. Next we discussed basic operations with signed numbers, including addition, subtraction, multiplication, and division. Then we discussed fractions and powers and roots. After this basic material, we discussed various arithmetic properties of real numbers. This was followed by a discussion of the proper order of operations and the use of grouping symbols to group numbers together. Then we showed how to evaluate variable expressions and introduced some basic terminology that students should know when working with algebraic expressions. A substantial part of the chapter concerned various operations with exponents. We then discussed various operations with polynomials, including addition, subtraction, multiplication, and division. Next we discussed techniques for solving equations and inequalities. The chapter ended with a discussion of how to solve various types of word problems. Your child is now ready to move on to some more advanced material in the next chapter.

9

Algebra II

In Chapter 4, we discussed the concepts of the least common multiple, the greatest common factor, and prime factorization. These concepts were important when working with fractions, and they are important for the subjects we will consider in this second chapter on algebra. At this point, you may want to go back and reread the first part of Chapter 4 on these subjects. As a brief refresher, consider the following:

To find the *prime factorization* of a positive integer, we find the product of factors that are all prime numbers. As we saw earlier, we can find all of the prime factors through the use of a factor tree.

To find the prime factorization of 24:

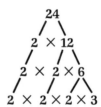

The prime factors of 24 are 2, 2, 2, 3

We could also do a prime factorization of the number 18 to find that its prime factors are 2, 2, 3.

The *greatest common factor* of two integers is the largest integer that is a factor of both numbers. For example, the greatest common factor of the numbers 18 and 24 is seen to be 6:

| | 18 | 24 | The greatest common |
| prime factors are: | $2 \cdot \underbrace{2 \cdot 3}_{6}$ | $2 \cdot 2 \cdot \underbrace{2 \cdot 3}_{6}$ | factor of 18 and 24 is 6. |

In a similar manner, we can also find the greatest common factor for an algebraic expression:

$$9x^3 - 15x^2 + 12x = (3 \cdot \underbrace{3 \cdot x} \cdot x \cdot x) - (5 \cdot \underbrace{3 \cdot x} \cdot x) + (2 \cdot 2 \cdot \underbrace{3 \cdot x})$$

The greatest common factor is 3x.

Emphasize to your child that she would not want to write out every algebraic expression in this fashion because it is very time consuming. Instead, she can write each prime factor as a power of itself. For the expression above:

$$9x^3 - 15x^2 + 12x = (3^2 \cdot x^3) - (5 \cdot 3 \cdot x^2) + (2^2 \cdot 3 \cdot x)$$

The greatest common factor is 3x.

To find the greatest common factor from an expression written in this manner, we should find the prime factors that are common to each term (like 3 and x) and then raise each prime factor to the lowest power it has in any of the terms. For example, the lowest power of 3 is 3^1, which occurs in the second and third terms; the lowest power of x is x^1, which occurs in the third term. The greatest common factor of this expression is the product of these powers; in other words, $3^1x^1 = 3x$, as shown above.

Factoring an Expression

The reason why the greatest common factor is so important is because you can use it to factor an expression. To find what is known as the polynomial factor, we divide each term of the expression by the greatest common factor. For the expression above:

$$\frac{9x^3}{3x} - \frac{15x^2}{3x} + \frac{12x}{3x} = 3x^2 - 5x + 4$$

The expression divided by the greatest common factor yields the polynomial factor.

Once your child has found the polynomial factor, he has everything he needs to factor the expression, because the product of the greatest common factor and the polynomial factor equals the expression:

$$9x^3 - 15x^2 + 12x = 3x\,(3x^2 - 5x + 4)$$

He can check that these are the correct factors of the expression by multiplying them together using the distributive property:

$$3x\,(3x^2 - 5x + 4) = 9x^3 - 15x^2 + 12x$$

Let's do another example using two variables to make sure that your student has mastered the approach. Suppose we want to factor the following expression, $28x^2y^2 - 14xy + 21x^2$:

$$28x^2y^2 - 14xy + 21x^2 = 2^2 \cdot 7x^2y^2 - 2 \cdot 7xy + 3 \cdot 7x^2$$

The greatest common factor is $7x$.

$$\frac{28x^2y^2}{7x} - \frac{14xy}{7x} + \frac{21x^2}{7x} = 4xy^2 - 2y + 3x$$

This is the polynomial factor.

$$28x^2y^2 - 14xy + 21x^2 = 7x\,(4xy^2 - 2y + 3x)$$

These are the two factors.

By multiplying these two factors together, using the distributive property, we can verify that they are the correct factors:

$$7x\,(4xy^2 - 2y + 3x) = 28x^2y^2 - 14xy + 21x^2$$

Students should also learn that another way to factor an expression is to rearrange its terms into smaller groups and find the greatest common factor of each group. This is often known as *factoring by grouping*. For example, we can arrange the following expression into two groups and find the greatest common factor of each group:

$$3x^2 - 6xy + 3x - 6y = 3x^2 - 6xy \qquad + 3x - 6y$$

greatest common   greatest common
factor = 3x   factor = 3

We can now factor each group using its greatest common factor:

$$= 3x\,(x - 2y) \qquad + 3\,(x - 2y)$$

greatest common factor = x − 2y

We can also factor both groups, since they have a greatest common factor:

$$= (x - 2y)\,(3x + 3)$$

This results in the factored expression:

$$3x^2 - 6xy + 3x - 6y = (x - 2y)\,(3x + 3)$$

Point out to your child that she can go one step further, since 3 can be factored out of the second group of the expression. This results in:

$$3x^2 - 6xy + 3x - 6y = 3\,(x - 2y)\,(x + 1)$$

At this point, the expression is fully factored.

One of the most common types of factoring students will use is *factoring the difference of two squares*. With this, as with other types of factoring, the trick is to recognize the form of the expression. For example, the difference of two squares is of the form: $x^2 - y^2$. This factors into the product of the sum and the difference of the two terms:

$$(x + y)(x - y) = (x + y)x + (x + y)(-y) \quad \text{by the distributive}$$
$$= x^2 + xy - xy - y^2 \qquad \text{property.}$$
$$= x^2 - y^2$$

Thus, the factors of the expression $x^2 - y^2$ are $(x + y)$ and $(x - y)$.

As an easy way to factor the difference of two squares, set up the blank form of the two factors, with one factor having a plus sign and the other having a minus sign:

one factor has a plus   one factor has a minus

$$x^2 - y^2 = \qquad (\ +\ ) \qquad\qquad (\ -\ )$$

Then:

Put the principal square root of the first term here.

$$x^2 - y^2 = \qquad (x + y) \qquad (x - y)$$

Put the principal square root of the second term here.

Let's try another example to make sure that you have mastered the approach. Factor the expression $16x^2 - 25y^4$. (Notice that the principal square root of $16x^2$ is $4x$; the principal square root of $25y^4$ is $5y^2$.

First set up the blank form of the two factors,

$$16x^2 - 25y^4 = (\ +\ )(\ -\ )$$

then insert the principal square roots in the proper places.

$$16x^2 - 25y^4 = (4x + 5y^2)(4x - 5y^2)$$

A difference of two squares, as in the examples shown above, is a binomial because there are two terms. You will also need to know how to *factor a trinomial*, which is an expression with three terms. Very often the multiplication of two binomials yields a trinomial, as in the following case:

$$(x + y) (x + y) = (x + y) x + (x + y) y \quad \text{by the distributive}$$
$$= x^2 + xy + xy + y^2 \quad \text{property.}$$
$$= x^2 + 2xy + y^2$$

Let's take a closer look at how these two binomials are multiplied together to yield a trinomial. As shown below, the first terms of the binomials are multiplied together to get the first term of the trinomial; the inner and outer products of the binomials are added together to get the middle term of the trinomial; and the last terms of the binomials are multiplied together to get the last term of the trinomial:

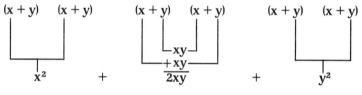

first term of the   middle term of the   last term of the
trinomial   trinomial   trinomial

This popular method of multiplication is called the FOIL method, because it stands for <u>F</u>irst + (<u>O</u>uter + <u>I</u>nner) + <u>L</u>ast. Knowledge of this method will come in very handy to students when we discuss how to factor trinomials. For now, let's apply the FOIL method to multiply two other binomials to get a trinomial, just to make sure that your youngster has mastered the technique. Multiply $(5x + 4)$ by $(7x - 3)$:

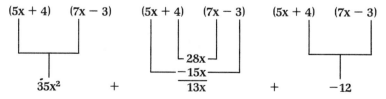

We are now ready to examine how to *factor a trinomial with a leading coefficient of 1*. To determine the leading coefficient, arrange the terms of the trinomial in order of descending powers. The coefficient of the term with the highest power is the leading coefficient. For example, find the leading coefficient of $-7x + x^2 + 10$:

$-7x + x^2 + 10$ in order of descending powers is $x^2 - 7x + 10$

leading coefficient = 1

Before we discuss how to factor this trinomial, notice that it is the product of two binomials. (You can check that the product of these two binomials equals the trinomial by multiplying them together using the FOIL method):

product of two binomials   trinomial

$(x - 5)(x - 2)$ $=$ x^2 $-$ $7x$ $+$ 10

last two terms of binomial⏌   first   middle   third
                                term   term   term

Notice that the product of the last two terms of the binomials equals the third term of the trinomial, $(-5) \cdot (-2) = (+10)$, and their sum equals the coefficient of the middle term of the trinomial, $(-5) + (-2) = (-7)$. This relationship is the key to factoring a trinomial into two binomials.

To factor the trinomial, $x^2 - 7x + 10$, you should proceed in the following manner. First write the principal square root of the trinomial as the first term of each of the two binomials:

$$x^2 - 7x + 10 = (x \quad)(x \quad)$$

Then ask yourself which two factors equal the coefficient of the third term of the trinomial when *multiplied* together and also equal the coefficient of the middle term of the trinomial when *added* together. With a little bit of mental arithmetic, the answer is readily found to be (-5) and (-2). We then plug these two factors into the two binomials to complete the problem:

$$x^2 - 7x + 10 = (x - 5)(x - 2)$$

Let's factor another trinomial to illustrate the approach. Find the factors of the trinomial, $x^2 + 3xy - 28y^2$. Since the principal square root of (x^2) is (x), write this as the first term of each of the two binomials:

$$x^2 + 3xy - 28y^2 = (x \quad)(x \quad)$$

Now notice that the product of the factors (-4) and $(+7)$ equals the coefficient of the third term of the trinomial, and their sum equals the coefficient of the middle term. Therefore, we plug these two factors into the two binomials but, in this case, we must also add a (y) because $(-4y)$ times $(+7y)$ equals $(-28y^2)$, the third term of the trinomial:

$$x^2 + 3xy - 28y^2 = (x - 4y)(x + 7y)$$

Have your child multiply the two binomial factors together, using the FOIL approach, to verify that they equal the trinomial expression.

Your student is now ready to examine how to *factor a trinomial with a leading coefficient greater than one*. The method of factoring in this case is similar to the previous one, although now we must consider the factors of the first term as well as the last term of the trinomial. For example, suppose we want to factor the trinomial, $25x + 7x^2 + 12$. As before, we first need to arrange the trinomial in order of descending powers:

$25x + 7x^2 + 12$ in order of descending powers is $7x^2 + 25x + 12$

As a first step, have your child make a blank form of the binomial factors and fill in all obvious information:

$$7x^2 + 25x + 12 = (?x + ?) \quad (?x + ?)$$

We know that the variable in each binomial must be x because it is the principal square root of the first term (x^2) in the trinomial. We also know that, using the FOIL approach, the inner and outer products of the two binomials must be equal to 25x, the middle term of the trinomial. The trick now is to find the correct set of factors so that the two binomials multiplied together equal the trinomial expression.

To find the correct set of factors, you should list all of the factors of the first and last coefficients of the trinomial expression:

Factors of the first coefficient of the trinomial expression.

Factors of the last coefficient of the trinomial expression.

$$7 = 1 \cdot 7$$

$$12 = 1 \cdot 12$$
$$= 2 \cdot 6$$
$$= 3 \cdot 4$$

Now, using trial and error, we should select the pairs of factors whose product of the first terms of the binomials equals the first term of the trinomial; the sum of the inner and outer products of the binomials equals the middle coefficient of the trinomial; and the product of the last terms of the binomials equals the last term of the trinomial.

Since there is only one pair of factors of the first coefficient of the trinomial, we can go ahead and plug them in right away:

$$7x^2 + 25x + 12 = (1x + ?) (7x + ?)$$

Then, we select the pair of factors of the last coefficient of the trinomial expression that, when multiplied together, yield the correct value for the middle term of the trinomial expression. After a few trials, we find that the correct factors are 3 and 4, respectively:

$$7x + 25x + 12 = (1x + 3) \quad (7x + 4)$$

$$21x$$
$$+4x$$
$$25x$$

By multiplying the binomial factors together, using the FOIL approach, you can verify that they are correct factors of the trinomial expression.

When factoring a trinomial expression with a leading co-efficient greater than 1, tell your student it is often a good strategy first to factor out the greatest common factor. This simplifies the subsequent steps. For example, in the following trinomial expression, we can factor out the greatest common factor $(4x^2)$ before proceeding with the rest of the factorization:

$$8x^4 - 24x^3 + 16x^2 = 4x^2 (2x^2 - 6x + 4)$$

We can now focus on factoring the trinomial expression, $2x^2 - 6x + 4$. As before, we set up the blank form of the binomial factors, and fill in the obvious information:

$$2x^2 - 6x + 4 = (?x - ?) \quad (?x - ?)$$

$$?$$
$$+?$$
$$-6x$$

We know that the variable x is in each binomial, and we also know that each binomial has a minus sign, since the middle term of the trinomial is negative and the last term of the trinomial is positive. Furthermore, we know that the sum of inner and outer products equals $-6x$.

Next list all of the factors of the first and last coefficients of the trinomial expression:

Factors of the first coefficient of the trinomial expression.

Factors of the last coefficient of the trinomial expression.

$$2 = 1 \cdot 2$$

$$4 = 1 \cdot 4$$
$$= 2 \cdot 2$$

Since there is only one pair of factors for the first coefficient of the trinomial expression, we can plug them in:

$$2x^2 - 6x + 4 = (1x - \text{?})(2x - \text{?})$$

Now we can select a pair of factors of the last coefficient of the trinomial expression that will yield the correct value for the middle term of the trinomial expression. Trial and error reveals that the correct factors are 2 and 2. Plugging them into the binomial factors yields:

$$2x^2 - 6x + 4 = (1x - 2)\quad(2x - 2)$$

$$-4x$$
$$+-2x$$
$$-6x$$

Returning to the original expression that we wanted to factor, we recall that we first factored out the greatest common factor, $4x^2$. Therefore, the total factorization of the expression is as follows:

$$8x^4 - 24x^3 + 16x^2 = 4x^2(2x^2 - 6x + 4)$$
$$4x^2(x - 2)(2x - 2)$$

This last example illustrates an important principle students should know about factoring. As a first approach, it is always a good idea to factor out a greatest common factor. Then check to see if the remaining expression falls into some of the standard types we have considered, such as factoring by grouping, factoring the difference of two squares, and factoring trinomials with leading coefficients equal to 1 and greater than 1. Sometimes more than one approach can be used to factor an expression. Always have your child check to see if a factor already obtained can be factored again. When an expression is factored completely, no additional factors can be obtained.

Solving Equations by Factoring

The subject of factoring receives a lot of attention in algebra because it has many important applications. One of the more important applications is the use of factoring to solve equations. In an earlier chapter we discussed the methods for solving first-degree—or linear—equations in which the highest-degree term had an exponent of one (for example, x). Factoring is often used to solve second-degree—or quadratic—equations in which the highest-degree term has an exponent of two (for example, x^2). In addition, factoring can be used to solve higher-degree equations, in which the highest-degree term has an exponent greater than 2.

Factoring is used to solve a polynomial equation, in which a polynomial is on one side of the equation and zero is on the other. For example, if I wish to solve the equation $x^2 - 6x = -8$, I must first express it as the polynomial equation, $x^2 - 6x + 8 = 0$. I can then factor the left side of the equation as follows:

$$x^2 - 6x + 8 = 0$$
$$(x - 2)(x - 4) = 0$$

In order for this statement to be true, either $(x - 2) = 0$ or $(x - 4) = 0$ or both $(x - 2)$ and $(x - 4) = 0$. This just says that if the product of two factors equals zero, then either one of the factors, or both of the factors, must be zero. Thus, to find the possible solutions to this polynomial equation:

If	$x - 2 =$	0		If	$x - 4 =$	0	
	$+ 2$	$+ 2$				$+ 4$	$+ 4$
then	x	$=$	2	then	x	$=$	4

Therefore, the two solutions to this equation are $x = 2$ and $x = 4$. To check that these are the correct solutions, we can plug them back into the equation:

If $x = 2$ *If* $x = 4$

$$(x - 2)(x - 4) = 0 \qquad (x - 2)(x - 4) = 0$$
$$(2 - 2)(2 - 4) = 0 \qquad (4 - 2)(4 - 4) = 0$$
$$(0) \quad (-2) = 0 \qquad (2) \quad (0) = 0$$
$$0 = 0 \qquad\qquad 0 = 0$$

Here is an example of how to use factoring to solve a higher-degree equation with three factors:

$$3x^3 - 6x^2 - 9x = 0$$
$$3x(x^2 - 2x - 3) = 0$$
$$3x(x - 3)(x + 1) = 0$$

For this statement to be true, one or more of the factors must be zero:

If	$3x = 0$		If	$x - 3 =$	0	If	$x + 1 =$	0
	$\dfrac{3x}{3} = \dfrac{0}{3}$			$+ 3$	$+ 3$		$- 1$	$- 1$
then	$x = 0$		then	x	$= 3$	then	x	$= -1$

Thus, the solutions to this equation are $x = 0$, $x = 3$, and $x = -1$. You can check that these are the correct solutions by plugging them back into the factored equation.

Here is another example that shows how to use factoring to solve a geometrical problem. Suppose that the width of a rectangle is 4 feet less than its length, and the area of the rectangle is 32 square feet. What are the dimensions of the rectangle? We have been given the following information:

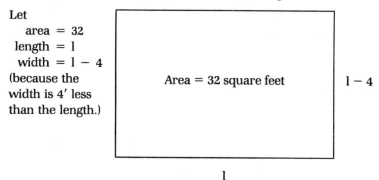

Let
 area = 32
 length = l
 width = l − 4
(because the
width is 4' less
than the length.)

Area = 32 square feet   l − 4

l

Now, since the area of a rectangle (32) equals its length (l) times its width (l − 4), we can express this information in the following formula:

$$\begin{array}{ccc} (l) & (l-4) = & 32 \\ \text{length} \times & \text{width} & \text{area} \end{array}$$

All we have to do now is multiply out the equation, and then put it into the form of a polynomial equation that we can factor:

$$l\,(l-4) = 32$$
$$l^2 - 4l = 32$$
$$l^2 - 4l - 32 = 0$$
$$(l - 8)\,(l + 4) = 0$$

If l − 8 =   0   If l + 4 =   0 ⎱ We can discard this
    + 8   + 8   − 4   − 4 ⎰ solution because it
then l   =   8   l   = − 4 ⎰ is impossible to have
                                        a negative length.

Therefore, the length (l) of the rectangle is 8 feet, and the width is (l − 4) or 4 feet. Multiplying the length by the width gives an area of 32 square feet, as stated in the problem.

Another important use of factoring is performing operations with algebraic fractions, as we will see in the next section.

Operations With Algebraic Fractions

Now that your child is familiar with ordinary fractions, it is a simple matter to understand algebraic fractions. Algebraic fractions have a numerator (n), a fraction line, and a denominator (d)—except now the numerator and denominator are polynomials. As before, values that make the denominator equal to zero are not allowed, because division by zero is not defined:

$\begin{array}{l} \text{n} \longleftarrow \text{numerator} \\ \text{—} \longleftarrow \text{fraction line} \\ \text{d} \longleftarrow \text{denominator} \end{array}$ $\left\{ \begin{array}{l} \text{where n and d are polynomials and no} \\ \text{value of d is allowed that will make} \\ \text{the denominator equal to zero.} \end{array} \right.$

Here are some examples of algebraic fractions:

$$\frac{x}{7}, \quad \frac{4}{x}, \quad \frac{6}{x-3}, \quad \frac{4x-7}{2x}, \quad \frac{x+8}{x^2-3x+2} = \frac{x+8}{(x-2)(x-1)}$$

$$\uparrow \qquad \uparrow \qquad \uparrow \qquad \qquad \uparrow \qquad \uparrow$$

$$(x \neq 0) \quad (x \neq 3) \qquad (x \neq 0) \qquad \qquad (x \neq 2, \quad x \neq 1)$$

You should remember from an earlier discussion that there are three signs associated with a fraction, and the same applies to algebraic fractions. The three signs are the sign of the numerator, the sign of the denominator, and the sign of the fraction itself. As before, you can change any two of the signs and the value of the fraction remains the same. Here is an example using algebraic fractions:

$$+\left(\frac{-4}{x}\right) = +\left(\frac{4}{-x}\right) = -\left(\frac{-4}{-x}\right) = -\left(\frac{4}{x}\right)$$

We say that fractions are *equivalent fractions* if they have the same value, even though they may initially look different. In this regard, it is important to realize that if a fraction is multiplied by another fraction that is equal to 1, then the value of the fraction remains the same. Here is an example:

$$\frac{4x + 3}{2x} = \frac{4x + 3}{2x} \cdot \frac{x}{x} = \frac{x (4x + 3)}{x (2x)} = \frac{4x^2 + 3x}{2x^2}$$

Multiplying this fraction by $\frac{x}{x}$ produces an equivalent fraction because $\frac{x}{x} = 1$.

Sometimes you will need to change the order of the terms in a binomial expression in order to perform algebraic operations. For example, all of the following binomial expressions are equivalent:

$$-(6 - x) = -1 (6 - x) = -6 + x = x - 6$$

A shorthand technique to remember is that whenever the terms of a binomial are interchanged, as above, the sign preceding the binomial expression is changed. For example, another way to express $(y - 4)$ is $-(4 - y)$. This technique is very useful for reducing fractions to their lowest terms.

Whether in arithmetic or algebra, we reduce fractions to their lowest terms because this makes it easier to work with them. To reduce algebraic fractions to their lowest terms, you should factor both the numerator and denominator completely and then rearrange the factors to form the same numerator and denominator. This enables you to cancel factors and reduce the fraction to its lowest terms. Here is an example:

$$\frac{8x^4y^3z^2}{4x^3y^2z} = \frac{2 \cdot 2 \cdot 2 \cdot x \cdot x \cdot x \cdot x \cdot y \cdot y \cdot y \cdot z \cdot z}{2 \cdot 2 \cdot x \cdot x \cdot x \cdot y \cdot y \cdot z} = 2xyz$$

Sometimes a higher-degree polynomial can be reduced to its lowest terms by factoring it into binomial factors:

$$\frac{3x^2 + 4x - 4}{x^2 + 9x + 14} = \frac{(3x - 2)\,\cancel{(x + 2)}}{(x + 7)\,\cancel{(x + 2)}} = \frac{3x - 2}{x + 7}$$

Here is an example in which rearranging the order of the terms in a binomial expression makes it easier to reduce an algebraic fraction to its lowest terms:

$$\frac{-(y - x)}{(x - y)} = \frac{\cancel{(x - y)}}{\cancel{(x - y)}} = 1$$

Just as we perform various types of arithmetic using ordinary fractions, we will find that it is necessary to perform various types of arithmetic using algebraic fractions. First we will discuss the *multiplication of algebraic fractions*. We multiply algebraic fractions in the same manner as ordinary fractions. First we factor both the numerator and denominator of the fraction. Then we rearrange the factors to form fractions with the same numerator and denominator, which we can cancel. And finally, we multiply the remaining factors in the numerator and divide them by the product of the remaining factors in the denominator to get the answer. Here are examples:

Example 1

$$\frac{24x^2}{7y^2} \cdot \frac{5y}{6x} = \frac{4 \cdot 6 \cdot x \cdot x}{7 \cdot y \cdot y} \cdot \frac{5 \cdot y}{6 \cdot x} = \frac{4 \cdot \cancel{6} \cdot \cancel{x} \cdot x \cdot 5 \cdot \cancel{y}}{\cancel{6} \cdot \cancel{x} \qquad 7 \cdot \cancel{y} \cdot y} = \frac{4 \cdot x \cdot 5}{7 \cdot y} = \frac{20x}{7y}$$

Example 2

$$\frac{3x^2}{x^2 - 7x + 12} \cdot \frac{3x^2 - 6x + 8}{x} = \frac{3xx}{(x - 3)(x - 4)} \cdot \frac{(3x - 2)(x - 4)}{x}$$

$$= \frac{3x\cancel{x}\,(3x - 2)\,\cancel{(x - 4)}}{\cancel{x}\,(x - 3)\,\cancel{(x - 4)}}$$

$$= \frac{3x\,(3x - 2)}{(x - 3)}$$

Students need to understand that we use the same technique to *divide algebraic fractions* that we use to divide ordinary fractions in arithmetic. When dividing two fractions, we first invert the second fraction and then proceed as in multiplication. Notice in the following examples that you can mentally rearrange the factors and perform the cancellations, thus saving yourself some steps:

Example 1

$$\frac{7x}{5y} \div \frac{3x^2}{15} = \frac{7x}{5y} \cdot \frac{15}{3x^2} = \frac{7x}{5y} \cdot \frac{15}{3x^2} = \frac{21}{3x} = \frac{7}{x}$$

Example 2

$$\frac{6x^2 - 9xy + 3y}{x^2 - y^2} \div \frac{6x - 3y}{x + y} = \frac{6x^2 - 9xy + 3y}{x^2 - y^2} \cdot \frac{x + y}{6x - 3y}$$

$$= \frac{(3x - 3y)(2x - y)}{(x + y)(x - y)} \cdot \frac{(x + y)}{3(2x - y)}$$

$$= \frac{(3x - 3y)}{3(x - y)} = \frac{3(x - y)}{3(x - y)} = 1$$

Adding algebraic fractions is also very similar to adding ordinary fractions in arithmetic. The simplest case is when you are adding like fractions, which means that they have the same denominators. In this case, all you have to do is add the numerators together and divide them by the denominator of the like fractions. As with ordinary fractions, the resulting fraction should be reduced to its lowest terms. Here are some examples:

Example 1

$$\frac{4}{x} + \frac{7}{x} = \frac{4 + 7}{x} = \frac{11}{x}$$

Example 2

$$\frac{3x}{x + y} + \frac{3y}{x + y} = \frac{3x + 3y}{x + y} = \frac{3\,\cancel{(x + y)}}{\cancel{(x + y)}} = 3$$

Sometimes algebraic fractions may not look like they have the same denominators, but you can make them like fractions by changing a sign. Here is an example:

$$\frac{6}{x - y} + \frac{5}{y - x} = \frac{6}{x - y} + \frac{5}{-(x - y)} = \frac{6}{x - y} + \frac{-5}{x - y} = \frac{6 - 5}{x - y} = \frac{1}{x - y}$$

In this example, we employed two operations that we learned before. First, we interchanged two terms in a binomial expression and changed the sign in front of them. Second, we changed two signs in a fraction. Both of these operations produced equivalent fractions, but now with the same denominators that we can add together.

Subtracting algebraic fractions is also very similar to subtracting ordinary fractions. If they are like fractions, with the same denominators, we change the sign of the numerator of the fraction being subtracted and then proceed as in the addition of algebraic fractions. As before, the numerator should be factored, and the resulting fraction should be reduced to its lowest terms. Here are examples:

Example 1

$$\frac{2}{3x} - \frac{8}{3x} = \frac{2}{3x} + \frac{-8}{3x} = \frac{2 - 8}{3x} = \frac{-6}{3x} = -\frac{\cancel{6}^{2}}{\cancel{3x}_{1}} = -\frac{2}{x}$$

Example 2

$$\frac{3x}{9x - 3y} - \frac{y}{9x - 3y} = \frac{3x}{9x - 3y} + \frac{-y}{9x - 3y} = \frac{3x - y}{9x - 3y}$$

$$= \frac{\cancel{(3x - y)}}{3\,\cancel{(3x - y)}} = \frac{1}{3}$$

In order to add and subtract unlike algebraic fractions, we have to find their *lowest common denominator*. The lowest common denominator is the smallest number that is divisible by each of the denominators. The lowest common denominator is just the least common multiple of the denominators, which we encountered before, because it is the smallest number that is a multiple of the denominators.

Let's do an example that shows your youngster how to find the lowest common denominator of two unlike fractions. Find the lowest common denominator of:

$$\frac{14}{12x^3y^2} \quad \text{and} \quad \frac{7}{4x^2y^3}$$

The first task is to factor the two denominators completely. Factors that repeat should be expressed as powers:

$$12x^3y^2 = 2^2 \cdot 3 \cdot x^3 \cdot y^2 \qquad 4x^2y^3 = 2^2 \cdot x^2 \cdot y^3$$

Next we write each different factor that appears in either denominator,

$$2, 3, x, y$$

and then raise it to the highest power that occurs in either denominator:

$$2^2, 3, x^3, y^3$$

To find the lowest common denominator, simply multiply all of these powers together:

$$2^2 \cdot 3 \cdot x^3 \cdot y^3 = 12x^3y^3$$

Here is another example to illustrate the approach. Find the lowest common denominator of:

$$\frac{4x}{(x^2 - y^2)} \quad \text{and} \quad \frac{3y}{x(x - y)^2}$$

First, factor the two denominators completely and express factors that repeat as powers:

$$(x^2 - y^2) = (x + y)(x - y) \qquad x(x - y)^2 \text{ is already factored.}$$

Then write each different factor that appears in either denominator and raise it to the highest power that occurs in either denominator:

$$(x + y), (x - y)^2, x$$

To find the lowest common denominator, multiply all of these powers together:

$$(x + y) \cdot (x - y)^2 \cdot x = (x + y)(x - y)^2 x$$

After getting some more experience working with unlike fractions, you should be able to find their lowest common denominator very quickly and easily.

Now that you know how to find the lowest common denominator, it is a straightforward task to *add unlike fractions*. First find their lowest common denominator. Next convert all of the fractions to equivalent fractions by multiplying them by any factors in the lowest common denominator that do not appear in their own denominator. Then simply add the resulting like fractions and reduce them to their lowest terms. Here are a couple of examples you can show your child to illustrate the approach:

To add $\frac{7}{x^2} + \frac{4x}{x^3}$, notice that the lowest common denominator is x^3. We can convert x^2 in the denominator of $\frac{7}{x^2}$ to the lowest common denominator x^3 in the following manner: $\frac{x}{x} \cdot \frac{7}{x^2} = \frac{7x}{x^3}$. Notice that $\frac{7x}{x^3}$ is an equivalent fraction to $\frac{7}{x^2}$ because we multiplied $\frac{7}{x^2}$ by $\frac{x}{x} = 1$, which does not change its value. Also note that we do not have to do anything to the fraction $\frac{4x}{x^3}$ because it already has the lowest common denominator x^3. Now we have two like fractions that we can add and simplify:

$$\frac{7}{x^2} + \frac{4x}{x^3} = \boxed{\frac{x}{x}} \cdot \frac{7}{x^2} + \frac{4x}{x^3} = \frac{7x}{x^3} + \frac{4x}{x^3} = \frac{7x + 4x}{x^3} = \frac{11x}{x^3} = \frac{11}{x^2}$$

Here is another example you can use, based on the same approach for adding unlike fractions:

To add $\frac{3x}{8x^2y} + \frac{4y}{28xy^2}$, notice that the lowest common denominator is $56x^2y^2$

To produce this lowest common denominator, we must multiply the fractions by the following factors,

$$\boxed{\frac{7y}{7y}} \cdot \frac{3x}{8x^2y} + \frac{4y}{28xy^2} \cdot \boxed{\frac{2x}{2x}} = \frac{21xy}{56x^2y^2} + \frac{8xy}{56x^2y^2}$$

and then combine and simplify them:

$$= \frac{21xy + 8xy}{56x^2y^2} = \frac{29xy}{56x^2y^2} = \frac{29}{56xy}$$

Now we will examine the approach for *subtracting unlike fractions*. The steps are essentially the same as in adding unlike fractions. As before, the only difference is that we must change the sign of the fraction being subtracted, and then proceed as in addition:

To subtract $\dfrac{7x}{x-y} - \dfrac{2y}{x+y}$, notice that the lowest common denominator is $(x-y)(x+y)$. To produce this lowest common denominator we must multiply the fractions by the following factors:

$$\boxed{\dfrac{(x+y)}{(x+y)}} \cdot \dfrac{7x}{x-y} - \dfrac{2y}{x+y} \cdot \boxed{\dfrac{(x-y)}{(x-y)}} = \dfrac{7x\,(x+y)}{(x+y)(x-y)} - \dfrac{2y\,(x-y)}{(x+y)(x-y)}$$

$$= \dfrac{7x\,(x+y)}{(x+y)(x-y)} + \dfrac{-2y\,(x-y)}{(x+y)(x-y)}$$

$$= \dfrac{7x^2 + 7xy - 2xy + 2y^2}{(x+y)(x-y)}$$

$$= \dfrac{7x^2 + 5xy + 2y^2}{(x+y)(x-y)}$$

You should show your child at least one more case involving the subtraction of unlike fractions, in the special case in which one of the numbers is a whole number. All of the same rules apply:

To subtract $8 - \dfrac{3x}{(x+y)}$, notice that the lowest common denominator is $(x+y)$. To produce this lowest common denominator, we multiply 8 by $\dfrac{(x+y)}{(x+y)}$. We don't need to do anything to $\dfrac{3x}{(x+y)}$, since it already has this denominator:

$$\boxed{\dfrac{(x+y)}{(x+y)}} \cdot 8 - \dfrac{3x}{(x+y)} = \dfrac{8\,(x+y)}{(x+y)} - \dfrac{3x}{(x+y)}$$

$$= \dfrac{8\,(x+y)}{(x+y)} + \dfrac{-3x}{(x+y)}$$

$$= \dfrac{8x + 8y - 3x}{(x+y)} = \dfrac{5x + 3y}{(x+y)}$$

All of the fractions you have shown your youngster so far are called simple fractions because they have one fraction line. *Complex fractions* have more than one fraction line, as illustrated in the following example:

Numerator of the complex $\Big\}$ $\dfrac{3}{x} + \dfrac{6}{x^2}$ $\Big\{$ Secondary fractions.
fraction.

Main fraction line. $\longrightarrow$ ——————

Denominator of the complex $\Big\}$ $2 + \dfrac{4}{x}$ $\Big\{$ Secondary fractions.
fraction.

There are two basic methods that can be used to simplify complex fractions. The first method is to multiply both the numerator and the denominator of the complex fraction by the lowest common denominator of all of the secondary fractions. We will illustrate this approach for the complex fraction shown above. In this problem, the lowest common denominator is x^2:

$$\frac{\dfrac{3}{x} + \dfrac{6}{x^2}}{2 + \dfrac{4}{x}} = \frac{x^2}{x^2} \cdot \frac{\dfrac{3}{x} + \dfrac{6}{x^2}}{2 + \dfrac{4}{x}} = \frac{x^2\left(\dfrac{3}{x} + \dfrac{6}{x^2}\right)}{x^2\left(2 + \dfrac{4}{x}\right)} = \frac{\dfrac{x^2}{1}\left(\dfrac{3}{x}\right) + \dfrac{x^2}{1}\left(\dfrac{6}{x^2}\right)}{\dfrac{x^2}{1}\left(\dfrac{2}{1}\right) + \dfrac{x^2}{1}\left(\dfrac{4}{x}\right)}$$

$$\frac{\dfrac{3x^2}{x} + \dfrac{6x^2}{x^2}}{\dfrac{2x^2}{1} + \dfrac{4x^2}{x}} = \frac{3x + 6}{2x^2 + 4x} = \frac{3\,(x + 2)}{2x\,(x + 2)} = \frac{3}{2x}$$

The second method is to simplify the numerator of the complex fraction and the denominator of the complex fraction, and then divide the simplified numerator by the simplified denominator. Here is an example of this approach to simplify the same complex fraction:

$$\frac{\dfrac{3}{x} + \dfrac{6}{x^2}}{2 + \dfrac{4}{x}} = \left(\frac{3}{x} + \frac{6}{x^2}\right) \div \left(2 + \frac{4}{x}\right) = \left(\frac{3x}{x^2} + \frac{6}{x^2}\right) \div \left(\frac{2x^2}{x^2} + \frac{4x}{x^2}\right)$$

$$= \frac{3x + 6}{x^2} \div \frac{2x^2 + 4x}{x^2} = \frac{3x + 6}{x^2} \cdot \frac{x^2}{2x^2 + 4x}$$

$$= \frac{3 \,(x + 2)}{2x \,(x + 2)} = \frac{3}{2x}$$

As you can see, both of these approaches yield the same result. Sometimes one of the approaches will make it easier to simplify a complex fraction than the other approach, but this depends on the type of problem. Either approach will work.

Now that your youngster knows how to simplify algebraic fractions, he or she is well on the way to knowing how to *solve equations with algebraic fractions*. The first task is to remove all fractions by multiplying each side of the equation by the lowest common denominator. Then you remove the grouping symbols, combine all of the like terms, and solve the resulting equation for the unknown value(s). As always, it is a good idea to check your solutions to make sure they are correct. To illustrate the approach, we will solve the following equation for the value of x:

$$\frac{2}{x - 4} + \frac{5}{x - 4} = 7$$

Multiply each side of the equation by the lowest common denominator, which is $(x - 4)$. This does not change the value of the equation.

$$\frac{(x - 4)}{1} \cdot \frac{2}{(x - 4)} + \frac{(x - 4)}{1} \cdot \frac{5}{(x - 4)} = \frac{(x - 4)}{1} \cdot \frac{7}{1}$$

Now remove the grouping symbols, combine the like terms, and solve the equation for x.

$$\frac{(x-4)}{1} \cdot \frac{2}{(x-4)} + \frac{(x-4)}{1} \cdot \frac{5}{(x-4)} = \frac{(x-4)}{1} \cdot \frac{7}{1}$$

$$2 + 5 = 7(x-4)$$
$$7 = 7x - 28$$
$$7 + 28 = 7x$$
$$35 = 7x \quad \text{or} \quad x = \frac{35}{7} = 5$$

You can check that $x = 5$ is the correct solution for this problem by plugging this value back into the original equation:

$$\frac{2}{x-4} + \frac{5}{x-4} = 7 \text{ implies } \frac{2}{5-4} + \frac{5}{5-4} = 7 \text{ or } \frac{2}{1} + \frac{5}{1} = 7$$

Notice in this problem that $x = 4$ would not have been an acceptable solution, because this would have implied division by zero. (The denominator is $x - 4$ and $4 - 4 = 0$, which is not allowed.)

Here is another example of solving an equation with algebraic fractions, when second-degree terms are present. Sometimes such equations can be solved by factoring, as in the following case:

$$\frac{3}{x} + \frac{2}{x-2} = 1$$

The lowest common denominator for this equation is $x(x-2)$. Multiply both sides of the equation by $x(x-2)$:

$$\frac{x(x-2)}{1} \cdot \frac{3}{x} + \frac{x(x-2)}{1} \cdot \frac{2}{(x-2)} = \frac{x(x-2)}{1} \cdot \frac{1}{1}$$

Now remove the grouping symbols, combine the like terms, and solve the equation for x:

$$\frac{\cancel{x}\,(x-2)}{1}\cdot\frac{3}{\cancel{x}} + \frac{x\,\cancel{(x-2)}}{1}\cdot\frac{2}{\cancel{(x-2)}} = \frac{x\,(x-2)}{\cancel{1}}\cdot\frac{\cancel{1}}{1}$$

$$3\,(x-2) + 2x = x\,(x-2)$$
$$3x - 6 + 2x = x^2 - 2x$$
$$5x - 6 = x^2 - 2x$$
$$0 = x^2 - 7x + 6$$
$$0 = (x-1)\,(x-6)$$

If either of these factors is 0, then we have a solution for this equation:

If $(x-1)=0$	If $(x-6)=0$
then $x=1$	then $x=6$

As a check, we can plug $x = 1$ and $x = 6$ back into the equation:

$$\frac{3}{x} + \frac{2}{x-2} = 1 \quad \text{implies} \quad \frac{3}{1} + \frac{2}{1-2} = 1 \quad \text{or} \quad 3 + (-2) = 1$$

$$\frac{3}{x} + \frac{2}{x-2} = 1 \quad \text{implies} \quad \frac{3}{6} + \frac{2}{6-2} = 1 \quad \text{or} \quad \frac{3}{6} + \frac{2}{4} = 1$$

Here again, make sure your child sees that $x = 0$ and $x = 2$ would not have been acceptable solutions, since they would imply division by 0.

Operations With Square Roots

We have already discussed square roots, so you should now know that the square root of a number is another number that, when multiplied by itself, equals the first number. You should also know that every positive number has both a negative and positive square root and that the positive square root is called the principal square root. For example, the positive (or principal) square root of 16 is 4, and the negative square root of 16 is -4. When these square roots are multiplied by themselves ($4 \cdot 4$ and $-4 \cdot -4$), the result is 16. As in the earlier part of this book, we will not be discussing the square root of a negative number (for example, $\sqrt{-1}$), which is called an imaginary number.

To discuss operations with square roots, it will be helpful if students understand some terminology. There are three key parts to a square root. For example, to express the square root of x:

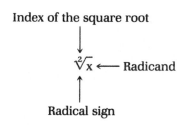

As a convention, the index of the square root (2) is not written, so the square root of x would be written just as $\sqrt{x}$. The radicand is the expression inside the radical sign.

There will be numerous occasions when students want to simplify square roots in order to make it easier to work with them. The first case we will consider is square roots where there are *no fractions present* in the radicand. Examples of these types of square roots include the following:

$$\sqrt{64} = 8 \text{ because } (8)^2 = 64 \qquad \sqrt{x^6} = x^3 \text{ because } (x^3)^2 = x^6$$

Notice that since finding the square root is the inverse of squaring, to find the square root of a number you divide the exponent of the radicand by 2. In the example above for $\sqrt{x^6}$, this means:

$$\sqrt{x^6} = x^{6 \div 2} = x^3$$

A rule that students will find very useful in working with square roots is the following (this applies to both numbers and letters):

$$\sqrt{x \cdot y} = \sqrt{x} \sqrt{y}$$

One application where this rule is immediately useful is finding the square root of a factor with an exponent that is an odd number. In this case, we can write the square root of the factor as the product of two factors, one with an even exponent and the other with an exponent of one. For example, to find $\sqrt{x^7}$:

$$\sqrt{x^7} = \sqrt{x^6 \cdot x^1} = \sqrt{x^6} \cdot \sqrt{x^1} = x^3\sqrt{x}$$

From the above rule, you should also be able to see that when a square root is multiplied by itself, the result is just the number that is the radicand:

$$\sqrt{x^2} = \sqrt{x \cdot x} = \sqrt{x} \cdot \sqrt{x} = x$$

When finding the square root of a number, it is a good idea to express it first as the product of prime factors. This makes it much easier to perform subsequent operations with the factor. Here are some examples:

$$\sqrt{72} = \sqrt{9 \cdot 8} = \sqrt{3^2 \cdot 2^3} = \sqrt{3^2 \cdot 2^2 \cdot 2^1}$$
$$= 3 \cdot 2\sqrt{2} = 6\sqrt{2}$$

$$\sqrt{18x^2y^3} = \sqrt{2 \cdot 3^2 \cdot x^2 \cdot y^3} = \sqrt{2 \cdot 3^2x^2y^2y^1}$$
$$3 \, x \, y \, \sqrt{2y}$$

The square root is considered to be simplified when no prime factor in the radicand has an exponent greater than or equal to 2, as in the above examples.

When fractions are present in the radicand, students need to know that some additional steps are necessary to simplify the square root. Not only must no prime factor in the radicand have an exponent greater than or equal to 2, but also no fractions can appear in the radicand and no denominator can have a square root. The following rule will be helpful in simplifying square roots with fractions present:

$$\sqrt{\frac{x}{y}} = \frac{\sqrt{x}}{\sqrt{y}}$$

We will now use this rule to simplify the following square roots with fractions:

$$\sqrt{\frac{5x^2}{16y^2}} = \frac{\sqrt{5x^2}}{\sqrt{16y^2}} = \frac{\sqrt{5}\,x}{4y} \qquad \sqrt{\frac{\overset{4}{\cancel{16}}x}{\underset{1}{\cancel{4}}y^2}} = \frac{\sqrt{4x}}{\sqrt{y^2}} = \frac{2\sqrt{x}}{y}$$

Sometimes you will end up with a square root in the denominator, and the denominator is an irrational number. (Remember from an earlier chapter that an irrational number is one that cannot be expressed in the form of $\frac{a}{b}$, whereas a rational number can be expressed in this form.) In such cases, we need to change the denominator into a rational number, a procedure known as *rationalizing the denominator*. Here is an example of rationalizing $\sqrt{3}$ in the denominator, which is an irrational number:

$$\sqrt{\frac{16x^2}{3}} = \frac{\sqrt{16x^2}}{\sqrt{3}} = \frac{4x}{\sqrt{3}} \cdot \frac{\sqrt{3}}{\sqrt{3}} = \frac{4\sqrt{3}\,x}{3} = \frac{4}{3}\sqrt{3}\,x$$

As you can see, we were able to remove $\sqrt{3}$ from the denominator by multiplying the whole expression by $\frac{\sqrt{3}}{\sqrt{3}}$, which equals 1. This does not change the value of the expression, but results in a denominator of 3, which is a rational number.

Students need to know that they can use a similar approach to rationalize fractions in which the square root of a letter (literal) appears in the denominator. Here is an example:

$$\sqrt{\frac{9y^2}{x}} = \frac{\sqrt{9y^2}}{\sqrt{x}} = \frac{3y}{\sqrt{x}} \cdot \frac{\sqrt{x}}{\sqrt{x}} = \frac{3\sqrt{x}\,y}{x}$$

We are now ready to consider arithmetic operations with square roots. If you want to *multiply square roots*, you can use a rule that you have already learned, but in a slightly different way:

$$\sqrt{x\,y} = \sqrt{x}\,\sqrt{y} \quad \text{implies} \quad \sqrt{x}\,\sqrt{y} = \sqrt{x\,y}$$

All this says is that if you want to multiply two or more radicands under separate radical signs, you can multiply all of the radicands together under one radical sign. As before, you can then simplify the result. Here are some examples illustrating the approach:

Example 1

$$\sqrt{2x}\,\sqrt{8x} = \sqrt{2x \cdot 8x} = \sqrt{16x^2} = 4x$$

Example 2

$$\sqrt{3x^2}\,\sqrt{6y} = \sqrt{3x^2 \cdot 6y} = \sqrt{18x^2y} = \sqrt{2 \cdot 9 \cdot x^2y} = 3x\sqrt{2y}$$

To *divide square roots*, we can also apply a rule learned earlier, with a slight variation:

$$\sqrt{\frac{x}{y}} = \frac{\sqrt{x}}{\sqrt{y}} \quad \text{implies} \quad \frac{\sqrt{x}}{\sqrt{y}} = \sqrt{\frac{x}{y}}$$

We can now apply this rule to divide and simplify square roots. Here are two examples:

Example 1

$$\frac{\sqrt{32x^2}}{\sqrt{2x^4}} = \sqrt{\frac{32x^2}{2x^4}} = \sqrt{\frac{16}{x^2}} = \frac{\sqrt{16}}{\sqrt{x^2}} = \frac{4}{x}$$

Example 2

$$\frac{4\sqrt{25x^2}}{5\sqrt{2x}} = \frac{4}{5} \cdot \sqrt{\frac{25x^2}{2x}} = \frac{4}{5} \cdot \frac{\sqrt{25x}}{\sqrt{2}} = \frac{4}{5} \cdot \frac{5\sqrt{x}}{\sqrt{2}} \cdot \frac{\sqrt{2}}{\sqrt{2}}$$

$$= \frac{\overset{2}{\cancel{4}}}{\underset{1}{\cancel{5}}} \cdot \frac{\overset{1}{\cancel{5}}}{\underset{1}{\cancel{2}}}\sqrt{2x} = 2\sqrt{2x}$$

Now you can show your youngster how to *add square roots* together. The simplest case is where the square roots are like square roots, which means that they have the same radicand. This just says that the information under the radical sign is the same. In this case we simply add their coefficients, and multiply this sum by the like square root. Here are two examples to illustrate the approach:

$$5\sqrt{3} + 2\sqrt{3} = 7\sqrt{3} \qquad \frac{\sqrt{7}}{3} + \frac{2\sqrt{7}}{3} = \frac{1}{3}\sqrt{7} + \frac{2}{3}\sqrt{7} = 7$$

When adding unlike square roots you should simplify each square root that appears in the sum. Sometimes they turn out to be like square roots after simplification, and you can add them as in the above examples. If they truly are unlike square roots you cannot add them, but you can figure out their value using a calculator that has a square root key. Here are some examples:

Adding like square roots after simplification	Unlike square roots that can not be added.

$$4\sqrt{7} + 2\sqrt{63}$$
$$= 4\sqrt{7} + 2\sqrt{9 \cdot 7}$$
$$= 4\sqrt{7} + 2 \cdot 3\sqrt{7}$$
$$= 4\sqrt{7} + 6\sqrt{7}$$
$$= 10\sqrt{7}$$

$$3\sqrt{5} + 8\sqrt{28}$$
$$= 3\sqrt{5} + 8\sqrt{4 \cdot 7}$$
$$= 3\sqrt{5} + 8 \cdot 2\sqrt{7}$$
$$= 3\sqrt{5} + 16\sqrt{7}$$

You can *subtract square roots* in the same manner. Here are two examples involving the subtraction of like square roots:

Example 1

$$8\sqrt{2} - 6\sqrt{2} = 2\sqrt{2}$$

Example 2

$$\frac{4\sqrt{3}}{3} - \frac{1\sqrt{3}}{3} = \frac{3\sqrt{3}}{3} = \sqrt{3}$$

If the square roots seem to be unlike, see if you can simplify and subtract them. Otherwise, you can figure out their value with a calculator.

Subtracting like square roots after simplication.	Unlike square roots that cannot be simplified.

$$7\sqrt{5} - 2\sqrt{20}$$
$$= 7\sqrt{5} - 2\sqrt{4 \cdot 5}$$
$$= 7\sqrt{5} - 2 \cdot 2\sqrt{5}$$
$$= 7\sqrt{5} - 4\sqrt{5}$$
$$= 3\sqrt{5}$$

$$8\sqrt{7} - 2\sqrt{27}$$
$$= 8\sqrt{7} - 2\sqrt{9 \cdot 3}$$
$$= 8\sqrt{7} - 2 \cdot 3\sqrt{3}$$
$$= 8\sqrt{7} - 6\sqrt{3}$$

Often in algebra you will have the need to *solve radical equations*, in which an unknown value appears under the radical sign. Here are some examples:

$$\sqrt{x} = 6 \qquad \sqrt{3x + 9} = 6 \qquad \sqrt{2x - 4} + 1 = 5$$

To solve radical equations such as these, the first task is to arrange the terms so that the radical is by itself on one side of the equation and all of the other terms are on the other side of the equation. Then square both sides of the equation. (As long as we do the same thing to both sides of the equation, we have not changed its value.) Finally, collect like terms and then solve the equation for the unknown value. It is always a good idea to check your solution in the original equation to make sure it is accurate. We will look at an illustration for each of the examples above.

The first example is the simplest case because the radical is already by itself on one side of the equation. All we have to do is square both sides of the equation to get the solution:

Solve:

$$\sqrt{x} = 6$$
$$x = 36$$

Check:

$$\sqrt{x} = 6$$
$$\sqrt{36} = 6$$
$$6 = 6$$

The second example requires a few more steps to get a solution. The radical is already by itself on one side of the equation, so we square both sides. But then we have to move 9 to the other side of the equation and divide by 3 to solve for x:

Solve:

$$\sqrt{3x + 9} = 6$$
$$3x + 9 = 36$$
$$3x = 36 - 9$$
$$x = \frac{27}{3} = 9$$

Check:

$$\sqrt{3x + 9} = 6$$
$$\sqrt{3(9) + 9} = 6$$
$$\sqrt{27 + 9} = 6$$
$$\sqrt{36} = 6$$
$$6 = 6$$

The third example is similar to the first but requires one additional step. We need to move 1 to the other side of the equation so the radical will be by itself. Then we can proceed as in the second example:

Solve: Check:

$$\sqrt{2x - 4} + 1 = 5$$

$$\sqrt{2x - 4} = 5 - 1$$

$$\sqrt{2x - 4} = 4$$

$$2x - 4 = 16$$

$$2x = 20$$

$$x = \frac{20}{2} = 10$$

$$\sqrt{2x - 4} + 1 = 5$$

$$\sqrt{2(10) - 4} + 1 = 5$$

$$\sqrt{20 - 4} + 1 = 5$$

$$\sqrt{16} + 1 = 5$$

$$4 + 1 = 5$$

$$5 = 5$$

One last example is worth looking at, because it involves the situation where the unknown value x appears on both sides of the equation. An example of this type is:

$$\sqrt{7x + 2} = x + 2$$

We can solve this equation by using the factoring technique developed earlier.

Solve: Check:

$$\sqrt{7x + 2} = x + 2$$

$$7x + 2 = (x + 2)^2$$

$$7x + 2 = x^2 + 4x + 4$$

$$0 = x^2 - 3x + 2$$

$$0 = (x - 2)(x - 1)$$

If x = 2

$$\sqrt{7x + 2} = x + 2$$

$$\sqrt{7(2) + 2} = 2 + 2$$

$$\sqrt{16} = 4$$

$$4 = 4$$

If x = 1

$$\sqrt{7x + 2} = x + 2$$

$$\sqrt{7(1) + 2} = 1 + 2$$

$$\sqrt{9} = 3$$

$$3 = 3$$

Solving Quadratic Equations

Quadratic equations are polynomial equations in which the highest-degree term is the second degree, and for this reason they are also called second-degree equations. We encountered such equations earlier and learned how to solve them by factoring. We will now examine several other methods for solving quadratic equations.

The general form of a quadratic equation is:

$$ax^2 + bx + c = 0 \qquad \text{where a, b, and c are real numbers.}$$

You can put any quadratic equation into the general form by carrying out the following steps. First remove any fractions by multiplying both sides of the equation by the lowest common denominator. Next remove any grouping symbols and combine all like terms. Then arrange all of the terms in order of descending powers on one side of the equation, leaving only zero on the other side. Here is an example:

Quadratic equation | General form

$$5 = -3x^2 + 4x \qquad 3x^2 - 4x + 5 = 0$$

$$a = 3 \quad b = -4 \quad c = 5$$

Here is another example in which a term is missing:

Quadratic equation | General form

$$7x^2 = 8 \qquad 7x^2 + 0x - 8 = 0$$

$$a = 7 \quad b = 0 \quad c = -8$$

To remove fractions, multiply both sides of the equation by the lowest common denominator (8):

Quadratic equation | General form

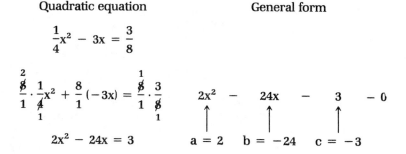

$$\frac{1}{4}x^2 - 3x = \frac{3}{8}$$

$$\frac{\overset{2}{\cancel{8}}}{1} \cdot \frac{1}{\cancel{4}}x^2 + \frac{8}{1}(-3x) = \frac{\overset{1}{\cancel{8}}}{1} \cdot \frac{3}{\cancel{8}} \qquad 2x^2 - 24x - 3 - 0$$

$$a = 2 \quad b = -24 \quad c = -3$$

$$2x^2 - 24x = 3$$

Earlier we examined how to solve a quadratic equation by factoring. It will be useful to re-examine the approach here.

To solve a quadratic equation by factoring, first put the equation into the general form. Then factor the polynomial and set each factor equal to zero to solve for the unknown values. As always, it is a good idea to check the solutions in the original equation to make sure they are accurate. Here is an example:

$x^2 - 5x = -4$	Original quadratic equation.
$x^2 - 5x + 4 = 0$	General form of the quadratic.
$(x - 4)(x - 1) = 0$	Factor the quadratic.

To find the solutions: *Check for $x = 4$:*   *Check for $x = 1$:*

$$x^2 - 5x + 4 = 0 \qquad x^2 - 5x + 4 = 0$$

$x - 4 = 0 \qquad x - 1 = 0 \qquad (4)^2 - 5(4) + 4 = 0 \qquad (1)^2 - 5(1) + 4 = 0$

implies $x = 4$ implies $x = 1$ $16 - 20 + 4 = 0 \qquad 1 - 5 + 4 = 0$

When a quadratic equation is in the general form and either b or c (or both) is zero, then we have an *incomplete quadratic equation*. It is not possible for a to be zero, because the equation would not be quadratic. Here are some examples of incomplete quadratic equations:

$4x^2 - 7 = 0$	$8x^2 - 2x = 0$	$10x^2 = 0$
(b = 0)	(c = 0)	(b and c = 0)

We will now consider how to solve a quadratic equation when c = 0. The proper approach is to find the greatest common factor and then solve the equation by factoring. We can see how this works for the above example:

$8x^2 - 2x = 0$	(c = 0) in this equation.
$2x(4x - 1) = 0$	The greatest common factor is 2x.

If $2x = 0$,   *If $4x - 1 = 0$,*   Find the values of x that

then $x = 0$ then $4x = 1$ make the equation equal to

and $x = \dfrac{1}{4}$ zero.

To show how to solve a quadratic equation when b = 0, we first have to introduce the symbol "$+/-$", which is read "plus or minus." This concept comes in handy when discussing the square root of a number, because the square root of a number can be either a positive or a negative number. For example, the square root of 9 is either a positive 3 (the principal square root) or a negative 3. We would write this as follows:

$$\sqrt{9} = \pm 3 = +3 \text{ or } -3$$

To solve a quadratic equation when b = 0, the first task is to rearrange the equation so the second-degree term is on one side and the constant term (c) is on the other. To illustrate, we would arrange the above example as follows:

Rearrange $4 x^2 - 7 = 0$ to become $4 x^2 = 7$

The next task is to divide both sides of the equation by the coefficient (a) of x^2, in this case 4:

$$\frac{4x^2}{4} = \frac{7}{4} \quad \text{becomes} \quad x^2 = \frac{7}{4}$$

Now, to get x on one side of the equation and everything else on the other side, all we have to do is take the square root of both sides of the equation, which does not change the value of the equation:

$$\sqrt{x^2} = \pm\sqrt{\frac{7}{4}} \quad \text{implies} \quad x = \pm\sqrt{\frac{7}{4}} = \pm\frac{\sqrt{7}}{\sqrt{4}} = \pm\frac{\sqrt{7}}{2}$$

Notice that there is both a positive and negative solution to this problem, because either value equals a positive $\frac{7}{4}$ when multiplied by itself. Also notice that if the term under the radical sign (the radicand) was a negative number, the solution would not be a real number. The square root of a negative number is called an imaginary number.

Your youngster can use the techniques I have presented above to solve some quadratic equations, but there is a formula known as the *quadratic formula* that can be used to solve *any* quadratic equation. To use the quadratic formula, the first task is to put the quadratic equation into its general form:

$$ax^2 + bx + c = 0$$

The quadratic formula gives a way to solve for x based on the following relationship of the coefficients a, b, and c:

$$x = \frac{-b \pm \sqrt{b^2 - 4ac}}{2a}$$

To solve for x in any given quadratic equation, all you have to do is substitute the coefficients for a, b, and c into the quadratic formula. As always, you should simplify your answers and check their accuracy by substituting them back into the original equation. Let's do an example to illustrate the approach:

Solve the equation $3x^2 + 9x - 12 = 0$ Notice that $\begin{cases} a = & 3 \\ b = & 9 \\ c = & -12 \end{cases}$

Now substitute these values into the quadratic equation:

$$x = \frac{-b \pm \sqrt{b^2 - 4ac}}{2a} = \frac{-9 \pm \sqrt{(9)^2 - 4(3)\,(-12)}}{2(3)}$$

$$= \frac{-9 \pm \sqrt{81 + 144}}{6} = \frac{-9 \pm \sqrt{225}}{6}$$

$$= \frac{-9 \pm 15}{6} = \begin{cases} = \dfrac{-9 + 15}{6} = \dfrac{6}{6} = 1 \\ \\ = \dfrac{-9 - 15}{6} = \dfrac{-24}{6} = -4 \end{cases}$$

Thus, the solutions to this problem are x = 1 and x = −4. To check that these solutions are accurate, we can plug them back into the original equation:

Check	$3x^2 + 9x - 12 = 0$	
If x = 1:	$3(1)^2 + 9(1) - 12 = 3 + 9 - 12 = 0$	
If x = −4:	$3(-4)^2 + 9(-4) - 12 = 48 - 36 - 12 = 0$	

Summary

In this second chapter on algebra you have been introduced to several additional topics. We showed how to use the greatest common factor to factor an expression. We then discussed a number of techniques for factoring expressions, such as factoring by grouping, factoring the difference of two squares, and factoring trinomials with a leading coefficient equal to 1 and greater than 1. We then saw how to solve an equation by factoring. Following this, we moved to a discussion of operations with algebraic fractions, including multiplication, division, addition, and subtraction. We then showed how to find the lowest common denominator to add and subtract unlike fractions. From there, we covered operations with complex fractions and showed how to solve equations with algebraic fractions. Operations with square roots were covered in detail, including multiplication, division, addition, and subtraction. The chapter ended with a discussion of how to solve quadratic equations, including the use of factoring, techniques for solving incomplete quadratic equations, and application of the quadratic formula.

10

Graphing Equations

It is much easier for students to understand algebraic relationships in a graph, because they can see a picture of them. Actually, your child saw the first step in producing a graph when we discussed the horizontal number line in an earlier chapter. If we draw another number line vertically and place its zero point at the zero point of the horizontal number line, then these two lines together form the axes of the rectangular coordinate system. We refer to the horizontal axis as the x-axis, the vertical axis as the y-axis, and the point where the two lines intersect as the origin:

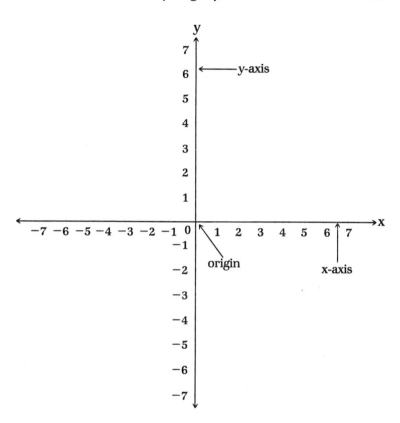

Explain to your child that the horizontal and vertical axes together form a plane in the rectangular coordinate system. With only a horizontal number line, we represented a single number by a point on the number line. With a rectangular coordinate system, we represent a pair of numbers by a point in the plane. We call this pair of numbers an ordered pair, such as (2,5), in which the first number is the horizontal x-coordinate, and the second number is the vertical y-coordinate. What this says is that we should move 2 units to the right and 5 units up to plot the point, as shown below:

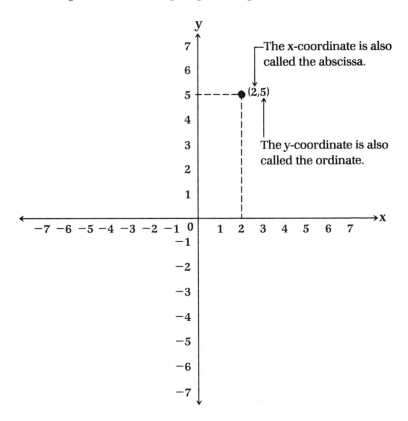

Show your child that all x-coordinates to the left of the vertical axis are negative, whereas all x-coordinates to the right of the vertical axis are positive. You should also show your child that all y-coordinates below the horizontal axis are negative, and all y-coordinates above the horizontal axis are positive. Now your child should be able to see that the intersection of the two axes divides the plane into four quadrants, and the quadrant in which a point is located depends on whether its x- and y-coordinates are positive or negative:

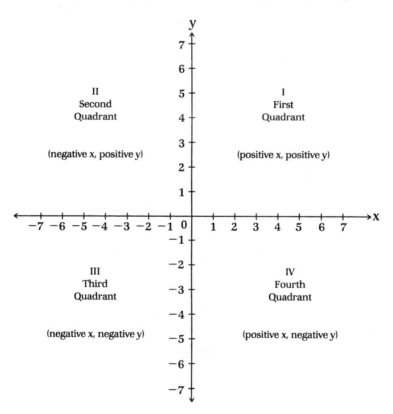

You should illustrate these basic concepts to your child by showing him or her how to plot several sample points. For example, to plot the point (3,4), in the first quadrant, move three units to the right, and four units up. To plot the point (−3,4), in the second quadrant, move three units to the left and four units up. To plot the point (−2,−5), in the third quadrant, move two units to the left and five units down. Finally, to plot the point (5,−6), in the fourth quadrant, move five units to the right and six units down. You may want to see if your child can plot several additional points to reinforce the concept.

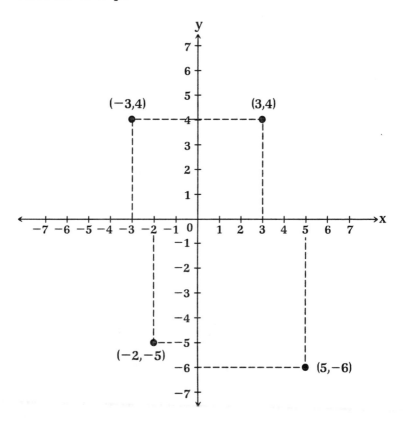

Graphing Straight Lines

The next thing to show youngsters is that they can plot not only points on a graph but also lines as well. Suppose, for example, that we want to graph the equation $y = x + 2$, which is a straight line. (First-degree equations with no more than two variables are called linear equations, and their graph results in a straight line.) To graph this equation, we must find values of x and y that make the equation true. The way to do this is to select sample values of x, plug them into the equation, and solve for y. This will result in a set of ordered pairs that lie on the line. Although you only need to find two points to determine a straight line, it is often useful to find three or four to make sure that the calculations are correct. You can use the following table of values to show your child how to find some ordered pairs that lie on the straight line:

The equation is $y = x + 2$ Table of values

x	y
−1	1
0	2
2	4
4	6

When x = −1,   y = −1 + 2 = 1
When x =   0,   y =   0 + 2 = 2
When x =   2,   y =   2 + 2 = 4
When x =   4,   y =   4 + 2 = 6

Now that we have determined a set of ordered pairs that satisfies the equation, we can plot them on a graph. To plot the straight line, all we have to do is draw a line through all of the points. If one of the points does not lie on the line, and it is a first-degree equation, you should go back and check your arithmetic. You can now show your child how to plot the straight line that corresponds to the equation $y = x + 2$:

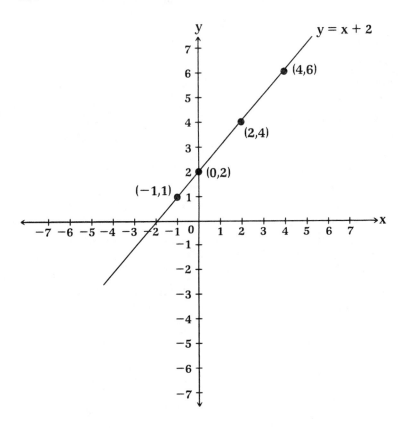

So your child will not be confused, you should show him or her how to plot a straight line with an equation that initially may look a little bit different and that points in a different direction. Consider the equation 6x + 3y = 12. We can solve this equation for y before constructing the table of values:

$$6x + 3y = 12$$
$$3y = -6x + 12$$
$$y = -2x + 4$$

Now show your child how to construct a table of values for the equation:

The equation is $y = -2x + 4$ Table of values

x	y
-1	6
0	4
1	2
3	-2

When $x = -1$, $y = -2(-1) + 4 = 6$
When $x = 0$, $y = -2(0) + 4 = 4$
When $x = 1$, $y = -2(1) + 4 = 2$
When $x = 3$, $y = -2(3) + 4 = -2$

And then plot the equation based on this set of ordered pairs:

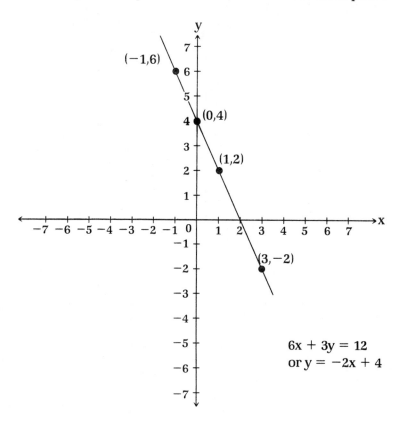

$6x + 3y = 12$
or $y = -2x + 4$

Another important concept to explain to children is that some equations of a straight line have only one variable. For example, if we plot the line x = 5, this is a vertical line made up of all of the points that have an x-coordinate equal to 5. If we plot the line y = −3, this is a horizontal line made up of all of the points that have a y-coordinate equal to −3. The two lines are shown in the graph below, along with a few sample points that are on the line. Actually, there are an infinite number of points along these lines, as long as they have the properly designated x or y values. You may want to ask your child to show you a couple of additional vertical or horizontal lines for practice.

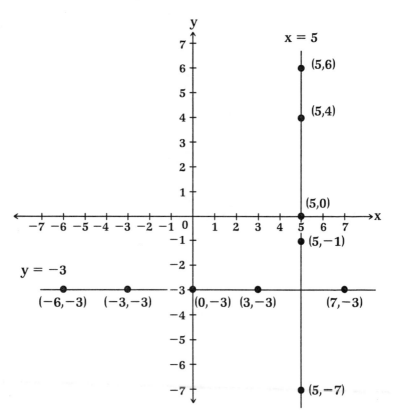

Finding the Intercepts

If your child has asked you which points to use when plotting the graph of a straight line, the answer is that any set of points will do; however, some points are more instructive than others. Two points of special interest are where x and y equal zero. Consider the following example:

The equation is y = −3x + 6

Table of values

x	y
0	6
2	0

When x = 0, y = −3 (0) + 6 = 6
When y = 0, 0 = −3x + 6 or −6 = −3x
                                        2 = x

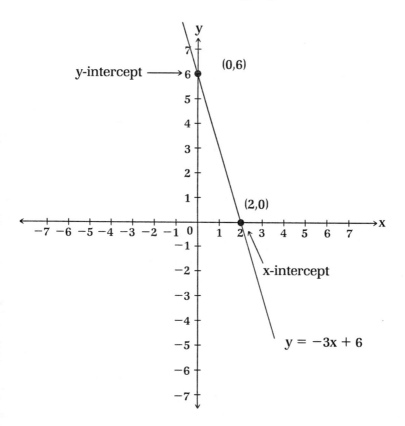

Point out to your child that when x = 0, this determines the point (0,6) where the straight line meets the y-axis (also known as the y-intercept). Also point out that when y = 0, this determines the point (2,0) where the straight line meets the x-axis (also known as the x-intercept).

It is very important to know how to find the intercepts of a straight line, so let's consider one more example that is a special case:

The equation is y = x   Table of values

x	y
0	0
4	4

When x = 0,   y = 0. Also, when y = 0, x = 0.
When x = 4,   y = 4

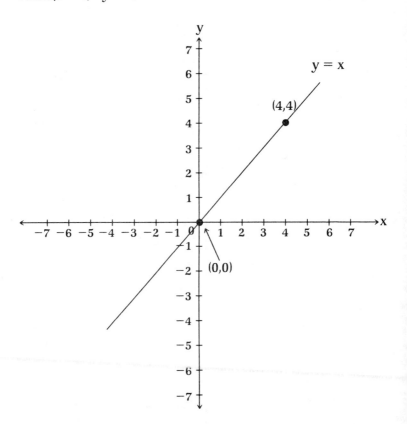

Finding the Slope

Another important concept to understand is the slope, or steepness, of the line. The slope is defined as follows:

$$\text{Slope} = \frac{\text{change in y}}{\text{change in x}}$$

This simply says that as we move from one point on the line to another point, we can find the slope by dividing the change in y values by the change in x values. To illustrate the concept, suppose we move from one arbitrary point P_1 (x_1, y_1) to another arbitrary point $P_2 = (x_2, y_2)$ along a given line:

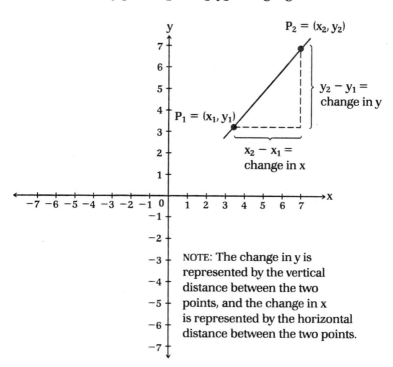

NOTE: The change in y is represented by the vertical distance between the two points, and the change in x is represented by the horizontal distance between the two points.

This says that the slope equals the change in y values (called the rise) divided by the change in x values (called the run). For the example above, the slope (sometimes referred to as m), can be written as:

$$\text{Slope} = \frac{\text{change in y}}{\text{change in x}} = \frac{\text{rise}}{\text{run}} \quad \text{or} \quad m = \frac{y_2 - y_1}{x_2 - x_1}$$

Now you can show how to calculate the slope of a line that runs through two specific points, say $P_1 = (-2, -3)$ and $P_2 = (2,5)$:

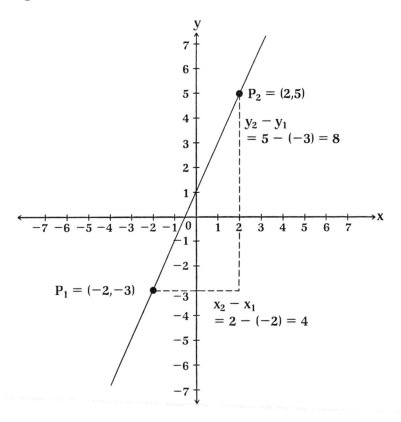

To find the slope, simply divide the difference in y by the difference in x:

If $P_1 = (-2,-3)$, then slope (m) $= \dfrac{y_2 - y_1}{x_2 - x_1} = \dfrac{5 - (-3)}{2 - (-2)} = \dfrac{8}{4} = 2$
$P_2 = (2,5)$

It is important to impress upon students that the slope would not be changed if we reversed points P_1 and P_2:

If $P_1 = (2,5)$, then slope (m) $= \dfrac{y_2 - y_1}{x_2 - x_1} = \dfrac{-3 - (5)}{-2 - (2)} = \dfrac{-8}{-4} = 2$
$P_2 = (-2,-3)$

Another example will show that lines that slope downward have a negative slope:

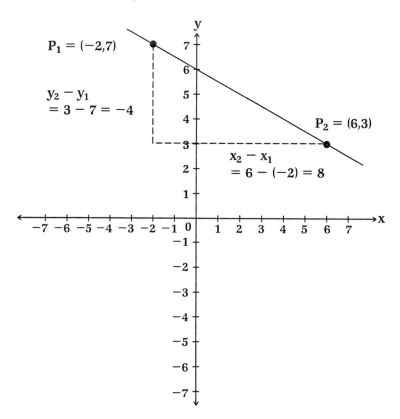

Here again, to find the slope of this line we merely divide the difference in y by the difference in x:

If $P_1 = (-2,7)$, then slope (m) $= \dfrac{y_2 - y_1}{x_2 - x_1} = \dfrac{3 - (7)}{6 - (-2)} = \dfrac{-4}{8} = \dfrac{-1}{2}$
$P_2 = (6,3)$

Students also need to know how to find the slope of a horizontal line and that the slope of a vertical line is undefined. To illustrate these concepts, you can show them the graph below:

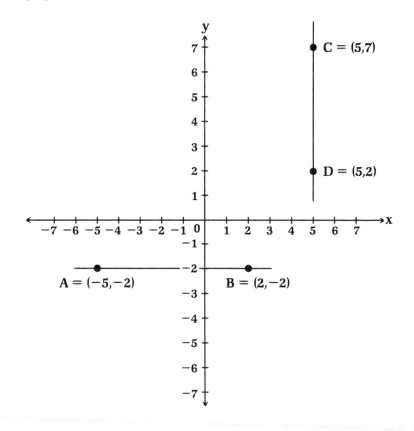

By calculating the change in y over the change in x for the two points along the horizontal line, we see that its slope is 0:

If A $= (-5, -2)$, then slope (m) $= \dfrac{y_2 - y_1}{x_2 - x_1} = \dfrac{-2 - (-2)}{2 - (-5)} = \dfrac{0}{7} = 0$
  B $= (2, -2)$

The slope of a vertical line is not defined because we cannot divide by 0, as shown in the following example:

If C $= (5, 7)$, then slope (m) $= \dfrac{y_2 - y_1}{x_2 - x_1} = \dfrac{2 - (7)}{5 - (5)} = \dfrac{-5}{0}$ which is undefined
  D $= (5, 2)$

Equations of a Straight Line

It is important to be able to recognize and express different forms of equations for a straight line. Any first-degree equation with no more than two variables is an equation of a straight line. The *general form* of such equations can be written as follows:

$Ax + Bx + C = 0$ where A, B, and C are real numbers and B and C are not both equal to 0.

To put equations into their general form, it is desirable for A to be positive and A, B, and C to be expressed as integers. Here is an example you can show to illustrate the concept:

$\dfrac{1}{2}x - \dfrac{3}{4}y = 2$ can be multiplied by 4 (the lowest common denominator) to become $\underset{\uparrow}{2x} - \underset{\uparrow}{3y} - \underset{\uparrow}{8} = 0$
                                                                                                                A   B   C

Another form of an equation for a straight line that students should know about is the *point-slope form*. To introduce this concept, we can return to the formula for slope (m) discussed earlier, with one slight modification. We now want the two points on the line to be expressed as $P_1 = (x_1, y_1)$ and $P = (x, y)$ to be any other point on the line.

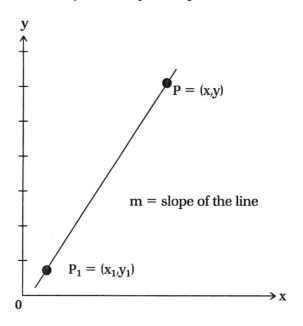

We can now express the formula for slope as:

$$m = \frac{y - y_1}{x - x_1}$$

If we now multiply both sides of this equation by $(x - x_1)$, which does not change the value of the equation, we get:

$$(x - x_1)\, m = \frac{y - y_1}{x - x_1} (x - x_1) \qquad \text{or} \qquad y - y_1 = m\,(x - x_1)$$

This latter expression is known as the point-slope form of the equation of a straight line, where m is equal to the slope and $P_1 = (x_1, y_1)$ is a known point on the line.

It is important to show that one can use this formula to find the general form of the equation of a straight line if he or she knows its slope and only one point on the line. For example, if the slope of a straight line is 3 and a point on the line is (5,9), find the general form of the equation:

Point-slope form   Substitute in known values   General form

$$y - y_1 = m (x - x_1) \qquad y - 9 = 3 (x - 5) \qquad 3x - y - 6 = 0$$
$$y - 9 = 3x - 15$$
$$y = 3x - 6$$

You are now ready to show your child the most commonly used form of an equation for a straight line, known as the *slope-intercept form*. The common tradition is to use the letter b to represent the y-intercept of the line. Thus, the point (0,b) is a point on the line:

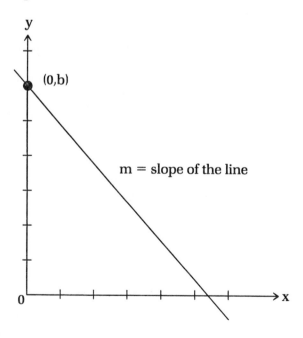

All we have to do now is plug this specific point (0,b) back into the point-slope form of equation for a straight line:

$$y - y_1 = m (x - x_1) \qquad \text{Point-slope form.}$$
$$y - b = m (x - 0) \qquad \text{Plug in point (0,b).}$$
$$y - b = mx \qquad \text{Multiply the terms.}$$
$$\text{or} \qquad y = mx + b \qquad \text{Rearrange the terms.}$$

Thus, the slope-intercept form of an equation for a straight line is $y = mx + b$, where m is the slope and b is the y-intercept. Now you want to show that one can use this form of equation to do some practical things.

As a first example, you can use this form to find the equation of a line when you know the slope and y-intercept of the line. Suppose, for example, that the slope is -3 and the y-intercept is -5. To find the general form of the equation, first plug these values into the slope-intercept form, then rearrange the equation:

$$y = mx + b \qquad \text{Write slope-intercept form.}$$
$$y = -3x - 5 \qquad \text{Plug in values.}$$
$$3x + y + 5 = 0 \qquad \text{Rearrange into general form.}$$

As a second example, you can show your child how to determine the slope from an equation given in general form:

$$12x + 3y - 9 = 0 \qquad \text{General form of the equation.}$$
$$3y = -12x + 9 \qquad \text{Rearrange the terms.}$$
$$y = -4x + 3 \qquad \text{Divide both sides by 3.}$$

It is now easy to find the slope and y-intercept from the slope-intercept form of the equation:

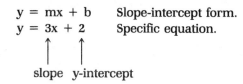

$$y = -4x + 3 \qquad \text{Slope-intercept form.}$$

slope   y-intercept

As a third example, you can show that one does not have to use a table of values to graph a straight line; he or she can use the slope-intercept form of an equation instead. Suppose the slope-intercept form of the equation is as follows:

$$y = mx + b \qquad \text{Slope-intercept form.}$$
$$y = 3x + 2 \qquad \text{Specific equation.}$$

slope   y-intercept

Remember from our earlier discussion that we can write the slope as follows:

$$\text{Slope} = \frac{\text{rise}}{\text{run}} = \frac{\text{change in y}}{\text{change in x}} = \frac{3}{1}$$

Thus, when x changes by 1 unit, y changes by 3 units.

Now, to graph this line, first we plot the y-intercept (0,2), and from this point move 1 unit to the right (in the x-direction) and up 3 units (in the y-direction) to plot a second point (1,5). Then draw a line through the two points:

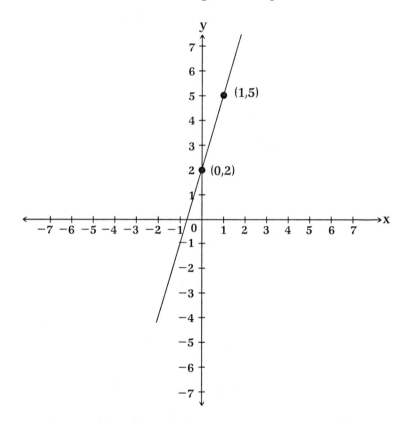

Here is one final example you can show to reinforce the concept. It involves the situation in which the slope is a fractional number and the y-intercept is negative. Graph the equation:

$$y = \frac{4}{5}x - 3$$

Notice that the slope is $\dfrac{4}{5}$ and the y-intercept is $(0, -3)$. The slope indicates that if x increases by 5 units, then y increases by 4 units. Thus, we can start at the point $(0, -3)$ and move 5 units to the right (in the x-direction) and up 4 units (in the y-direction) to plot the second point $(5,1)$. Then we merely draw a line to connect the two points:

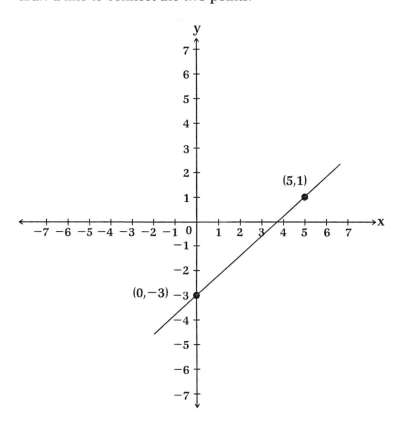

Graphing Curved Lines

Students know that not all lines are straight, so it is instructive to also show them how to graph curved lines. Unlike straight lines, which have first-degree (linear) equations with no more than two variables, the equations for curved lines are not linear. Thus, it is necessary to plot more than two points to graph the equation of a curved line.

Here are a couple of steps you should follow when plotting the graph of a curved line. The first step is to use the curve's equation to construct a table of values. Next, plot the points from the table of values. Finally, draw a smooth line through the points to trace out the graph. It is necessary to plot enough points to trace out the true shape of the curve. Here is an example of the approach for graphing a parabola, which has one of its variables as a squared term. Graph the equation $y = x^2 - 4$:

Value of x	Equation		Table of Values	
	$y = x^2 - 4$			
			x	y
If $x = -3$,	$y = (-3)^2 - 4 =$	5	-3	5
If $x = -2$,	$y = (-2)^2 - 4 =$	0	-2	0
If $x = -1$,	$y = (-1)^2 - 4 =$	-3	-1	-3
If $x = 0$,	$y = (0)^2 - 4 =$	-4	0	-4
If $x = 1$,	$y = (1)^2 - 4 =$	-3	1	-3
If $x = 2$,	$y = (2)^2 - 4 =$	0	2	0
If $x = 3$,	$y = (3)^2 - 4 =$	5	3	5

We have determined seven points for this curve. We could have determined either fewer or more points, but the points selected give us a good idea of what the curve looks like.

Now show how to plot the points from the table of values and sketch out a smooth line connecting all of the points:

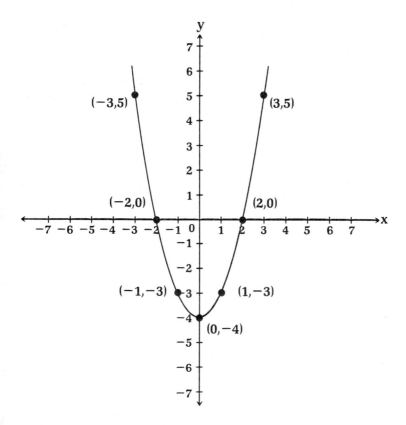

A similar approach will work when graphing other equations with higher-degree terms.

Graphing Inequalities

In an earlier chapter we discussed how to plot an inequality with one variable on a number line. Now you can show how to graph inequalities with no more than two variables in the plane formed by the rectangular coordinate system. In this section we will look at inequalities that divide the plane into two half-planes.

As an example, suppose you are asked to graph the inequality $3x - 6y \leqq 12$. As a first step, you should replace the inequality sign with an equality sign and plot the straight line. This can be done using the intercept method, where we find the value of y when x is equal to zero and find the value of x when y is equal to zero:

Equation	When $x = 0$	When $y = 0$	x	y
$3x - 6y = 12$	$3(0) - 6y = 12$	$3x - 6(0) = 12$	0	−2
	$-6y = 12$	$3x = 12$	4	0
	$y = -2$	$x = 4$		

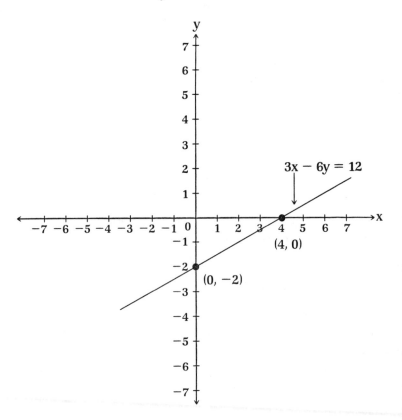

The line $3x - 6y = 12$ is called the boundary of the inequality because it divides the plane into two half-planes—half above the inequality and half below the inequality. To find out which half belongs to the inequality $3x - 6y \leq 12$, we plug in a value to see if it satisfies the inequality. Although any point can be selected, the point usually chosen is (0,0):

$$3x - 6y \leq 12$$
$$3(0) - 6(0) \leq 12$$
$$0 \leq 12$$

Thus, the point (0,0) and all other points in the half-plane above the boundary belong to the inequality, as shown by the shaded region below:

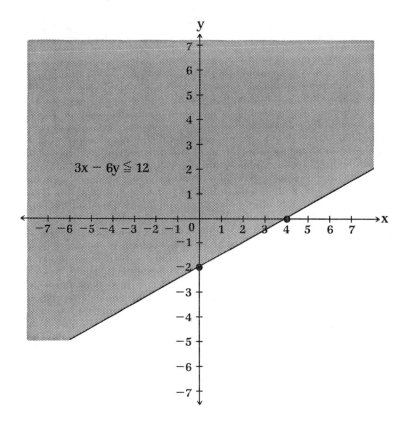

Point out that in the inequality $3x - 6y \leq 12$, the boundary is shown as a solid line and is included in the shaded region that belongs to the inequality. The boundary is included because the inequality sign is $\leq$. If instead the inequality was $3x - 6y < 12$, the boundary would be shown as a dotted line and would not be included in the shaded region that belongs to the inequality. The boundary would not be included because the inequality sign is $<$. The graph for the inequality $3x - 6y < 12$ is shown below:

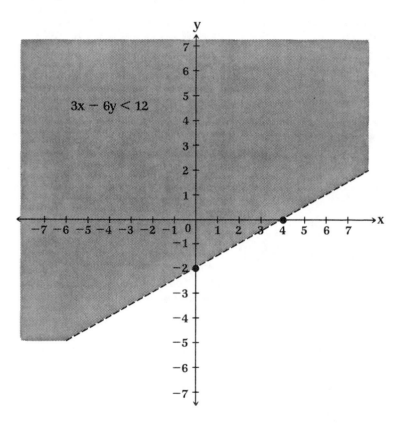

Summary

The ability to graph equations is an important skill for youngsters learning mathematics. These skills help them to see a physical representation of ideas being discussed, which enables them to develop a fuller understanding of the subject. As they advance to higher levels of mathematics, they will be able to use these skills to solve systems of equations and to graph a variety of different equations beyond those we considered here. Graphing is an indispensable skill to have when working with functions, which are a precursor for learning calculus. The basic ideas of calculus are usually taught using graphing representations. Graphing is also very useful when learning about the various trigonometric functions. A student who learns the proper methods of graphing at an early age will have much less difficulty later on with more advanced topics in mathematics. Parents can help in this regard by sitting down with their children and showing them the mechanics of graphing covered in this chapter.

11

Conclusion

In this book we have covered most of the topics normally encountered by students in elementary and junior high (middle) school. We started off with a discussion of basic arithmetic, decimals, and fractions. Then we moved to a discussion of practical concepts, such as ratios, proportions, and percents. Next we reviewed weights and measures, paying particular attention to the metric system. This was followed by a discussion of basic concepts in geometry, including various geometric figures and the measurement of perimeter, area, and volume. Substantial attention was devoted to algebra, in two separate chapters, since it is such an important subject for so many applications in mathematics. Finally, we concluded with a discussion of equations and graphing, since a knowledge of these subjects is required for understanding topics in higher mathematics, such as functions and calculus.

The discussion throughout has been directed to parents, since it is assumed that they will sit down with their children and explain the various concepts covered here. The material has been presented in a very structured manner, in easy-to-understand language, so the concepts will be readily accessible to children even before they encounter them in school. Each topic builds on an understanding of the previous topic, so it is best to work through the book in a sequential way. Parents have no doubt noticed that we have covered in one small book what normally requires a separate lengthy textbook for each year during the first eight or nine years of school. This is because we have not discussed all of the topics covered in school, only the major ones needed to understand the material presented in school. Moreover, I have only presented enough examples to enable students to understand the basic concepts and have not included the various practice exercises and homework problems normally found in textbooks. My goal has been to provide children with enough knowledge so they will understand the material when they encounter it in school.

This said, parents should realize that I have given them a tool to help their children understand and enjoy the subject of mathematics. Parents can progress through this book at a pace that seems comfortable to their children. By starting with children when they are very young, parents can present material in a manner that children can understand well before the teacher covers the topics in class. This, no doubt, will create the impression in the teacher's mind that your child is very sharp. It will also give the child a lot of confidence because he or she can easily master a subject that proves vexing to other children. I have seen over and over that children—or, for that matter, adults—enjoy something more when they are good at it. Others notice their accomplishments, and this provides an incentive to do even better in the future. This experience can turn what is often regarded as a dreary and dreaded subject into the student's favorite subject in the curriculum.

Parents should not underestimate the importance of mathematics for the future success of their children. When children ask why they have to learn a subject that they will probably never use again, emphasize to them that mathematics is becoming ever more necessary in our rapidly advancing technological world. An understanding of math is absolutely essential for students who want to study a scientific or technical subject in high school or college. Without an understanding of mathematics, children can suffer repeated frustration with subjects in school and may be prevented from entering the college or curriculum of their choice. And when children become young adults and go out in search of interesting and financially rewarding jobs in a future labor market, they will find that their prospective employers will expect them to have a knowledge of mathematics, computers, and technical subjects. Without this knowledge, they will find themselves competing for the less challenging and lower-paying jobs that are available. It is a scenario that parents can help avoid by getting their children on the right track early.

Lao Tzu, the ancient Chinese sage, said "A journey of a thousand miles must begin with a single step." By listening to the advice given in this book, your children have begun the journey. My hope is that the material contained here will make the rest of the journey more interesting, understandable, and enjoyable.

Appendix A
Multiplication Table

	1	2	3	4	5	6	7	8	9	10	11	12
1	1	2	3	4	5	6	7	8	9	10	11	12
2	2	4	6	8	10	12	14	16	18	20	22	24
3	3	6	9	12	15	18	21	24	27	30	33	36
4	4	8	12	16	20	24	28	32	36	40	44	48
5	5	10	15	20	25	30	35	40	45	50	55	60
6	6	12	18	24	30	36	42	48	54	60	66	72
7	7	14	21	28	35	42	49	56	63	70	77	84
8	8	16	24	32	40	48	56	64	72	80	88	96
9	9	18	27	36	45	54	63	72	81	90	99	108
10	10	20	30	40	50	60	70	80	90	100	110	120
11	11	22	33	44	55	66	77	88	99	110	121	132
12	12	24	36	48	60	72	84	96	108	120	132	144

About the Author

Gordon W. Green, Jr., knows a lot about education. He received an A in every graduate course he took en route to receiving a Ph.D. in economics from The George Washington University in 1984. This accomplishment was quite remarkable, considering that Dr. Green was attending graduate school part-time in the evening, working more than full-time at his regular job, and taking care of home and family responsibilities at the same time. Even with this busy schedule, he had plenty of time for leisure activities.

Dr. Green attributes his success to a unique system of study that he developed, which he first reported on in his book, *Getting Straight A's*. Since it was originally published in 1985, *Getting Straight A's* has been advertised numerous times in *Parade* magazine and has helped hundreds of thousands of students earn higher grades in school. In 1992, the work was translated into Spanish as *Como Sacar Una A* and now enjoys distribution world-wide. In his next book, *Helping Your Child to Learn*, Dr. Green adapted his study methods so they apply to the needs of elementary and junior high school students.

Dr. Green is now chief of the Governments Division at the U.S. Bureau of the Census. He directs the preparation of financial and employment statistics for federal, state, and local governments across the country, as well as a wide variety of statistics on elementary, secondary, and post-secondary education and the criminal justice system. Before that, he was an assistant chief in the Housing and Household Economics Statistics Division at the Bureau of the Census, where he directed the preparation of the nation's official statistics on income distribution and poverty. His Ph.D. dissertation on wage differentials for job entrants received national atten-

About the Author

tion, including a front-page article in the *New York Times*, articles in several other newspapers and magazines, and an appearance on national television to discuss his findings. His work is widely published in government periodicals, magazines, and professional journals.